BEYOND THE SCOREBOARD

Learn It Through Youth Sports, Carry It Through Life

BEYOND THE SCOREBOARD

Learn It Through Youth Sports, Carry It Through Life

Dr. Nick Molinaro and Celeste Romano

Library of Congress Cataloging-in-Publication Data has been applied for

ISBN: 978-1-7334929-0-4

Cover and layout design by Pfeifer Design

Creative License Publishing, LLC.
https://www.creativelicensepublishing.com

"Whether you are a parent, an elite athlete, or an adult with a professional career, the information and tools presented in *Beyond the Scoreboard* are invaluable. I've covered many types of athletes with various upbringings; everyone is different, both physically and mentally. Dr. Nick so eloquently breaks down each individual's unique mental reactions in sport and how to address, nurture, and build strength in the most important muscle, the mind. An NFL player told me in an interview, "If we have athletic trainers on the sidelines in a game to tape our ankle, fix an injury to get us back out there, why aren't there psychologists right there on the sidelines too to immediately help us fix something in our minds?" In *Beyond the Scoreboard*, Dr. Nick is that psychologist with you on the sidelines teaching parents, coaches, and athletes ways to deal with pressure, expectations, overcoming failure, and achieving success while still enjoying sports".

  – Tina Cervasio, FOX 5 NY Lead Sports Anchor/Reporter, Host of "Sports Xtra"(Emmy Award Winning Sports Broadcaster with over 20-years experience as an on-air talent in Boston, New York and Nationally on CBS Sports Network, FOX Sports, Big Ten Network)

"Dr. Nick covers all of the bases in *Beyond the Scoreboard*. Combining his vast experiences of working with elite athletes on all levels, this is a "must read" for parents and athletes alike. Dr. Nick has provided a roadmap which will help parents avoid making the wrong turns. We all want what is best for those we love and it starts by reading *Beyond the Scoreboard!*"

  – Bob Papa, The Voice of the NY Giants and Golf Channel

"Dr. Nick is our 'go-to' guy for all things between the player's ears. Golfers, parents, and coaches love Nick's clear identification of the essence of the problem and his step by step approach to removing obstacles and forming great habits and processes. This is a big deal particularly in golf where performance is affected by so many variables, some real and many imagined. Nick's stories and real-life examples bring these concepts to life and his ability to illustrate with words is very evident in *Beyond the Scoreboard* which should be required reading for anyone guiding a youngster through sport and life."

  – Jane Filing, Founder, WomensGolf.com

DEDICATION AND ACKNOWLEDGMENTS

Dr. Nick Molinaro

My work as a professional psychologist has been significantly influenced by my career-long mentor, Dr. Anthony Palisi. He had varied experiences in careers ranging from being a principal, football coach, sports editor, author, psychologist, and graduate school professor. I first met Tony at Seton Hall University as a graduate student and shortly after I suffered a life-threating illness. During those difficult times he offered support, care, love, and continued to mentor me through my doctoral studies, even serving as member on my doctoral committee. After my graduation, he served as my supervising psychologist, where I learned the art of therapy and consultation. Much of my work, learnings, and successes are a direct result of his encouragement, support, and leadership. He has also served as a model professional and more importantly as a spiritual, God-loving man.

My wife, Joan Milani, has remained supportive and encouraging throughout this process. I've never been easy to live with as she can certainly attest to. Not to mention that during the period of working on this book, there was additional stress placed on both my career and relationship. Her patience, care, and support have always been freely given. Her love is always offered unconditionally.

The inspiration for *Beyond the Scoreboard* comes from its co-author, Celeste Romano. Not only was she the initiator of this collaboration, but she remained at the helm of the three-year-long journey to its completion. Her spirit, insight, intuition, and creativity facilitated the process of discovery in writing our first book and assuredly not our last.

I wish to thank MK Brosnan for her assistance during the final stages in preparation of our book. She has served Celeste and me with organizational skills and assistance in the essentials of citations and figures. She has also acted as a "sounding board" to crystallize concepts and provide clarity for the reader. MK will remain as an assistant in my future works for presentations, research, and hands-on work with athletes, coaches, and teams.

DEDICATION AND ACKNOWLEDGMENTS

Celeste Romano

This book is dedicated to my boys, Alex and Zach, who inspire me every day with their dogged pursuit of their own dreams; no mother could be prouder. And for Craig, whose unwavering love and support I couldn't do without. I love you all beyond words.

First and foremost, I would like to thank Dr. Nick for listening to my pitch for this book three years ago. His willingness to take this idea and see it to fruition with me has been a gift. The countless hours and dedication to reach our goal added to his already packed schedule, but he never wavered in his determination and commitment to this book.

I would like to thank Liz, Paula, Kathy, Nana, Donna, Brian, Glenn, and Ken for their support throughout the entire writing process. I will be forever grateful for their insight, encouragement, and critiques.

I would also like to thank our editors, Elena and Julie. They have added immeasurable value to our work, and I thank them for challenging us to create the book we envisioned from the start.

And a huge thank you to Kris of Pfeifer Design for her incredible cover design and the formatting of our final copy. We are forever grateful for her patience, creativity, and support. I know this will be one of many projects we will work on together.

TABLE OF CONTENTS

FOREWARD

As a parent, professional golfer, instructor, Director at the Michael Breed Golf Academy, former host of "The Golf Fix" on the Golf channel, as well as my work on SiriusXM PGA Tour Radio, and Fox 5 Sports, the one truth I've learned is that every player struggles at some point with their mental game. I have the privilege of working with many talented players in golf and some who have gone on to win on the PGA tour, Web.com Tour, LPGA tour, and mini tours. And many, many times I've witnessed the impact of the mental game on performance. As a player, coach, or parent of a player, when the mental game falters, the answers we are looking for are not always available. And for some, the cost of a good sport psychologist is beyond their means. Well, that struggle is about to end after you read this book.

Like most athletes, I experienced a time when I struggled with my own mental game; something I couldn't fix on my own. So, I called on the services of sport psychologist, Dr. Nick Molinaro. Dr. Nick is a skilled sport psychologist who works with many professional, Olympic, collegiate (coaches, players and teams), and junior competitive athletes. Having worked with other sport psychologists in the past, I realized early on that Dr. Nick's approach was different. Dr. Nick doesn't recite platitudes or promise quick fixes to his players. Instead, he puts them to work identifying the stumbling blocks and limitations they place on themselves. He then gives them specific changes to make or tasks to perform in order to push them past their limits. None of these "fixes" are one-time cures; they are life-long changes that will take time and repetition to embed in an athlete's mind. And for those who have listened—myself included—they have had amazing results. Dr. Nick is the real deal.

One of the most common complaints I get from players and parents is that the player can't take the practice to the course or competition. Meaning, they can hit amazing shots on the range, but on the course, they fall apart—the beautiful practice shots become poor shots when they matter. Why? Because their mental game is failing them, not their physical game. On the practice range there is no pressure, the player is relaxed, and their mind is empty. Yet, when they walk onto the course, their mind is filling with other thoughts, mostly negative. Dr. Nick explains to parents and coaches how to take their players from practice to competition without negative thoughts or worries affecting their performance. Dr. Nick helps players by introducing pressure in practice and teaching them techniques to increase their attention which increases the level of performance when it matters—something I call "practicing with a purpose." I promise you it works. This is just a little taste of what you will learn from this book.

Working with young athletes, I deal with many parents. What I've come to realize over the years is that most parents, like myself, just want the very best for our kids. So, when I read this book, I did so as a coach and a parent. Almost immediately I recognized how impactful this information is for parents and coaches everywhere. Dr. Nick's co-author, Celeste Romano's anecdotal scenarios are on point and set the reader up for the information Dr. Nick will deliver in that chapter. As a reader you go from, "Oh, I get that," to "So, that's how I should handle it." And by the time you close the cover, you will take away critical information to help you support your child more effectively.

There is a way I instruct my players to hit the golf ball I call the "power angle." It's when the top line of the club comes down on the ball just ahead of the leading edge and it forces your hands forward. Striking the ball as such allows a golfer to gain more distance. And *Beyond the Scoreboard*, is the "power angle" for parents to help their young players get more distance out of youth sports and in turn other areas of their lives. Sports are a great way to teach kids life lessons they will carry with them forever. The longer they play, the more they learn. Dr. Nick teaches parents and players that if they think better, they will play better and enjoy more. Understand that playing better is not necessarily winning, but a player striving to reach their highest potential.

So, Let's do this.

– Michael Breed

PREFACE

Celeste Romano

It goes without saying that being a parent is challenging but add youth sports into the mix and life becomes a prodigious juggling act. Being a sport parent requires patience, organization, time, and dexterity. You need patience to encourage and foster your child's interest. Organization is imperative for juggling schedules, equipment, uniforms, and the dreaded carpools where you always seem to drive, and your car has its own lost and found section. Not to mention, the physical dexterity necessary to simultaneously handle kids, equipment, water bottles, clothing, and snacks, all while running to the field, usually located what feels like a million miles from your car. And that's before dealing with the sometimes-difficult personalities of other parents and coaches.

Yet, once you sit down to watch your little athlete, you secretly pray he has a good game. You end up sandwiched between the parents you wanted to avoid at all costs, the ones who spend the entire game criticizing the kids, coaches, and the refs. Somewhere around the sixth inning you want to stand up and yell at those negative parents, "I'm sorry I forgot you played for the Yankees before you decided to be a computer programmer!"

When you aren't dealing with the parents from hell in the stands, you may also be cursed with a bad-tempered coach. The man (or woman) who for all his efforts can't help but lose his patience with a group of six-year-olds—especially yours, because your child would rather play in the sand than on it. So, you suffer until the end of the season and celebrate your survival of it all like you just won the pennant.

Youth sports have morphed from recreational activities to being on par with and, in some instances, superseding academics. If a child shows any promise or passion for a sport, he or she is often pushed to specialize and compete in junior events or play on a club team. The idea of playing in college seems to be suggested to young athletes earlier and earlier. All this intensity has stolen much of the fun from athletics, causing our kids to leave organized sports at the staggering rate of 70% by age 13 (Miner, 2016).

If you have a child who makes it past the early years and then plays in high school, you have the ever-looming question of: "Will they play in college and beyond?" Not only do you ask your child that question, but all the other parents, coaches, and counselors are asking your child too. This can create a pressure cooker of stress, potentially killing any passion that once existed in the athlete. Your superstar might start to worry about their future in sports and what it all means for them.

Don't get me wrong. I, by no means, feel sports, pressure, or competition are bad. To the contrary, athletic competition—and the pressure that comes with it—teaches our athletes invaluable life lessons. So, an appropriate amount of each is not only good but necessary for building strong, confident, independent adults. It becomes problematic when the expectations are so high, they breed a level of pressure and competition that can be damaging for the athlete and parents alike.

When I think back to a few of my son's golf tournaments, they look a bit like this: On a jammed-packed practice green before every round I see them, the crazy dad hovering over his son as the kid tries to putt. The dad stands over his future Jordan Spieth, camera hanging from his shoulder, as he dictates instructions. Every missed putt receives criticism. Dad throws another ball back at the golfer to redo the shot.

My own son takes my elbow to his rib—a loving nudge, a wink-wink check-out-crazy-camera-guy-aren't-you-lucky-I'm-not-like-that? Yet, after several bogeyed holes, rummaging through fescue for the missed tee-shot, or three shots taken to get out of a bunker, his frustration skyrockets. That's when my crazy shows up. It appears on my face and in my lectures during the tense ride home. I declare that my child needs to learn to forget about the bad shots and move on. I continue to demand he keep his anger in check, and then scream at some driver who just cut me off. The message I want to deliver is lost—because I've become the crazy camera parent, without the camera.

I wonder, when all is quiet and my mind rummages through the good and bad points of a day like that: *Where are the days when it was just fun to watch my chubby-faced child swing a club? When did I open the door and let all the pressure walk inside? Am I really helping him to perform at his personal best in sport and in life?*

At the end of this particularly rough golf season, littered with mounting frustration and less than stellar tournaments, my 16-year-old and I sit quietly in the waiting room of Dr. Nick Molinaro, a highly regarded sport psychologist. My child's adolescent face, ever so quickly morphing into a man's, displays stress, tension, and a sprinkling of apprehension until the door opens and in walks a man who seems straight out of Central Casting. From his round horn-rimmed glasses and his fluffy white hair, to his argyle sweater vest, Dr. Nick embodies the quintessential psychologist, and soon, his demeanor reveals the special something that makes you want to sit on his couch and share every dysfunctional detail of your existence.

After Dr. Nick speaks with my athlete one-on-one, he calls me back in to his office. We immediately discuss how my child's anger affects his performance. How after an errant shot, his frustration begins and the snowball effect takes hold for several holes, all but sealing his fate of a negative outcome. And I ask: "How do I turn his attitude when he's given up? I keep telling him to forget that shot and move on."

Dr. Nick and my child exchange a glance before he turns to me: "When he feels frustrated by a bad shot, his feelings are appropriate and real. Telling him to ignore his feelings can make it more present. For example, if I tell you not to think about the pink elephant in the room, what will you think of?"

"A pink elephant."

"You see, what I explained to him is that he can have those feelings, but not while playing, since they are counter-productive. What he needs to do is recognize his negative emotions when they occur and then immediately table them. Put them aside to deal with later. But, do not pretend they don't exist. That will never work, just as the pink elephant example."

For me, this moment equates to sitting on Oprah's couch as she throws her hands straight up and yells, "Lightbulb moment!" (Cue the applause). I realize why all my attempts to shut down the negative emotions backfired. My dismissive attitude hasn't helped because it perpetuated my athlete's frustration, and it has made it all but impossible for him to recover. My athlete smiles at me, his way of assuaging my guilt and letting me know he's had his own lightbulb moment, that he too has some changes to make.

This proved to be only a morsel on the tip of the proverbial iceberg of information I wish I knew before I started on this sports journey with my child. I often wonder how different our experiences would have been if I had been armed with the critical information Dr. Nick imparted on us in the following months.

It wasn't until a conversation I had with some friends about our kids and youth sports that it hit me like an anvil to my head. Every parent, and every coach, needs wisdom from Dr. Nick to prepare them for the rigors of developing a young athlete's mental game and help kids get the most out of sports they can. And I'm not talking how to obtain a coveted scholarship, but how to make them higher performers in life overall. Shouldn't that be the goal?

My many conversations with Dr. Nick became the impetus to our collaboration on this book. We have presented the book as if you were sitting on Dr. Nick's soft brown leather couch, the gurgling fish tank directly across from you, as he addresses how to improve your athlete's mental game and maximize the benefits from sports. Whether your player is the next great baseball all-star or the worst player on the team, this book will help your athlete get the most out of his or her sports and apply what they learn in all areas of their life.

INTRODUCTION

Dr. Nick

If your car had engine trouble would you simply put new tires on it and expect it to have optimum performance? So, why have your athlete practice extensively, purchase them the best equipment, and monitor their nutrition, yet ignore their fears, anxiety, or mental blocks? No matter the emotional obstacle, it is strong enough to override any and all physical preparation for competition. Do not underestimate the power of the emotional game; it controls the physical performance at every turn. The common assumption that more confidence is all an athlete needs to eradicate fears or any other emotional struggle is factually incorrect. Confidence is not a cure.

Sports hold many opportunities for our young people to grow socially, physically, academically, and emotionally. However, constant pressure to be the best, pressure to specialize, fear of failure, and demanding schedules are consistently the causes for the athletic dropout rate. The staggering statistic that at least 70% of youths leave organized sports by the age of thirteen means that 70% of youths are missing the physical, social, and emotional benefits derived from participating in sports (Miner, 2016).

Every athlete is a sum total of talent, ability, personality, intelligence, culture, experiences, values, and parenting styles. How these components are nurtured in a youth is dependent on parental influence and directly affects an athlete's mental game. Note that for young athletes, parental influence is the greatest contributing factor to their environment. The mission of this book is to understand how the athlete's environment can positively impact the athlete's mental game. When the mental game is healthy, there will be a one-to-one correlation with performance in all aspects of life, not just athletics.

One of the most important and by far, the most difficult things we will do as humans is raise children. Albeit one of the most rewarding jobs, parenting truly is a day-to-day challenge. In addition to my career in psychology, I devoted many years working with youths and their parents. My most recent work centered on young athletes and their performance; in sport, academics, and interpersonal relations. In addition to my clinical work, I am also a father and grandfather. I fully understand the rigors that parents, teachers, and coaches experience in developing healthy, strong minds in our youths.

In my personal and professional experience, what always amazes me is how talented, young athletes dedicate themselves to their sport. Yet, with all that devotion, little to no focus is placed on their mental game, which is the athlete's true powerhouse. We often hear the term *powerhouse* in reference to one's core muscles. But the powerhouse that impacts both the emotional and physical performance of an athlete is the mind. The mind contains more power to influence an athlete's performance than any muscle in their body does, yet it is the most ignored area by athletes, coaches, and parents.

Popular methods, such as taping a few inspirational quotes to a gym wall, or reciting quotes to players, have little to no impact on a player's mental game. Yet, these continue to be the tactics coaches and parents use to try to emotionally prepare their athletes for competition. My years in sport psychology have led me to understand that most parents and coaches don't know how to effectively nurture the qualities necessary for an athlete to perform at their highest level.

Many self-help or inspirational books focus on the anomalies in our society—individuals that defy the odds—perpetuating the desire for our kids to be the next superstar. Our book is not about how to create the next Michael Jordan, Jordan Speith, or Derek Jeter. It's about helping your child develop critical mental skills for optimizing their performance in sports, which ultimately, transcends into all areas of their lives. We will help your athlete perform the very best they can. More importantly, each player will take away critical life skills. These skills will help them to perform at their highest level in whatever they do in life—sports related or not.

Why then focus solely on sports? Because sports are the quintessential vehicle for developing critical mental skills: grit, self-efficacy, and mindset. All of these attributes transfer into a child's overall life. Sports are a training ground for fostering emotional strength and the best way to measure one's performance under pressure.

Sports, I believe, are the only true measure of one's performance. For example, your child can get an A in English but does his or her A mean exactly the same thing as another child's A? Not really, because teachers, schools, classes, and programs all vary. In academics, no two As are the same. This is evident once your child gets to college. All the kids in the same college freshman class may have had similar GPAs in high school yet, some will do well, and others will struggle. Academic preparedness cannot be measured by one's report card. But, if you run a 7-minute mile, is it the same as another runner's 7-minute mile? Yes, it is.

In a world where individuals define themselves by what they do instead of who they are, there is a lack of understanding that who we are inside drives what we do. It's a sensitive dichotomy of emotions that ultimately makes each of us unique and makes us perform at such varying levels.

What makes one person excel against insurmountable odds and make another naturally gifted individual fail to deliver? The mind. Have you ever wondered what category you, your child, or the kids you coach fall into? Of course, 99% of us hope we are the individuals who deliver the win despite misfortune; that we are that person who defies the odds when downtrodden and with all-the-cards-stacked-against-us. Isn't that why we love those Hollywood feel-good movies where the underdog excels beyond every possible imagination? Yet when the rubber meets the road in our own lives, we often stumble and fall short. Why? Because we haven't tended to our mental game. We haven't developed the necessary mental attributes that others have, and that's why they've succeeded despite obstacles along the way.

Day in and day out, my office is a constant stream of individuals, many very athletically accomplished, struggling with something they can't get past. It's when they hit that proverbial wall that they show up seeking my help. Once we get to work, they usually realize that I don't fix their problem for them. I merely provide them with tools they can use to help themselves often with a simple shift of their perception. But not before we drill down to accurately define those perceptions and identify their internal beliefs.

Many of my most challenging clients come into my office looking for a quick fix, the proverbial one dose of "medicine" that will make their struggles go away. There is no such remedy. Acquiring mental strength takes work, time, and repetition. Few want to hear this, but for those that have listened and followed through, they've achieved excellence in their performance well beyond their expectations.

In this book, I will explain the attributes necessary for performance excellence as I would explain it to any client sitting in my office. This is not a quick fix book. You will have to do the work to help instill the critical attributes in your child. This is a life-changing exercise, not a one-time remedy. Just as having a healthy diet requires more than a good meal once in a while, mental strength requires constant nurturing. You will need to be brutally honest about yourself, your inner belief system, and your child to maximize the benefit of the information I'm sharing with you. You will need to define who you are inside, not what you do. Then you will need to do the same for your child. We can't change what we don't acknowledge as a problem or issue.

I caution you: this book is not purporting the idea that every child can become a world-class athlete. However, every child has the opportunity to achieve excellence under their own definition and get the most from a sport they can. Depending on the child, this could mean becoming a college athlete, a professional athlete, Olympic athlete, or simply being more active, or having fun with friends.

Together with Celeste Romano, a parent and a writer, I have synthesized critical information and put it in a user-friendly format to assist you in providing your child with the best environment for success. We will examine the coaching styles of parents who positively affected their athletes' success and what they did that set them apart from the pack. Conversely, negative parenting and coaching styles will be dissected and analyzed as well.

In addition to my expertise, this book compiles essential information from other successful, published works such as: Carol Dweck's *Mindset*, Angela Duckworth's *Grit*, and Daniel Coyle's *The Talent Code* to deliver a comprehensive guide to parents and coaches on supporting young athletes toward achieving excellence in sport.

Once you get real about yourself and your child, you will learn key attributes and how to adapt them to your child. After you're armed with all the critical base points, we will walk you through practice and performance. We'll tell you how you should handle practice and performance. What your child should be doing to achieve their goals with an emphasis on their goals. We will even give you vital information on dealing with coaches, other parents, and players during competition.

Athletic achievement is driven by one's mental strength, just as much as one's physical capabilities. We will provide necessary tools to encourage and promote your athlete's internal strength and fortitude.

We will share with you some very personal stories told by parents and athletes themselves that will serve as inspiration and, at times, cautionary tales. We will discuss athletes who walked away from a sport due to intense parental involvement, an athlete who lost his passion and could never get it back, and an athlete that made it despite all the odds against him. The common thread throughout is this: the athlete's success or failure hinges on their environment. Parents, you are the single greatest influence of your child's environment.

The information in this book will provide you with tools to avoid the pitfalls and create a wonderful experience in sports and life for your young athlete.

CHAPTER 1

Goodness of Fit

On Children

Your children are not your children
They are the sons and daughters of Life's longing for itself.
They come through you but not from you.
And though they are with you, they belong not to you.
You may give them your love but not your thoughts.
For they have their own thoughts.
You may house their bodies but not their souls,
For their souls dwell in the house of tomorrow,
Which you cannot visit, not even in your dreams.
You may strive to be like them, but seek not to make them like you.

—Khalil Gibran

It doesn't matter the sport or the age or level of your player; we have all witnessed that parent, the "crazy" one who berates their child openly. The parent who can't help but violently critique their kid to tears. The scene is awkward, and we almost always walk away patting ourselves on the back for not being that person. But I ask, could the seemingly small things we do or say to our athletes affect their mental game just as much as the "crazy" parents affect their own child?

For example: At the end of a devastating loss, you walk to the car as your athlete trudges behind, dragging themselves and their equipment, when you finally snap and say, "Buck up, it's life. Get over it and move on." You think you're being supportive and strengthening them emotionally. But are you? Could your dismissive reaction toward their feelings be incorrect or potentially damaging?

And then, let's suppose the athlete is very invested in a sport. They have specialized with a goal of playing in college. You go to their game and watch them completely unravel. You leave the sidelines shaking your head and expect your athlete to be as disappointed in their performance as you are, but they aren't. In fact, they are laughing and joking with friends like it never happened. And as your irritation spikes, you think, *Why, is he not angry at himself? This carefree attitude is telling me he's not fully committed and isn't feeling inspired to do better.* When you get home, you start your monologue on their poor performance, which you sprinkle with some cutting words, defined in your mind as "tough love." Will your anger and recrimination instill motivation or discouragement?

Have you ever asked yourself, "Could I make the negative experiences in sports more advantageous for my athlete? Could I address my own anxiety, or lack thereof, more appropriately so that he or she might learn from their mistakes rather than focus on my indifference or irritation? Are any struggles around his or her emotional game partly from my parenting?"

Dr. Nick

As parents, we harbor guilt about so many things we've done. Questioning our actions toward and about our children isn't just normal—it's healthy and demonstrative of responsible parenting. I always tell parents to go easier on themselves and to accept that, from time to time, they may fall short in doing the best for their child, despite their intentions. It's not an all or nothing game, but an iterative process of learning. When you fail, turn it around and do better next time. That's no different from what we teach our children.

Parents are the nucleus of their child's world from birth, taking care of all their needs, from the physical to emotional. Even during the teen years, when parents often feel invisible, they remain the epicenter of love and security for their offspring. Throughout these formative years, sports can be a significant part of a child's life. So, I emphasize to parents how crucial the symbiotic relationship is between the mind and body to inspire excellence in performance. I remind them that the environment they provide via their parenting style can positively or negatively impact their child's mental game and ultimately their physical game.

Let's examine the parent that thinks that degrading their child in front of the team and other parents is toughening them up, potentially inspiring them to do better. Most of us watch in horror at the scene. How has that harsh critique affected the athlete's mental game? Are they motivated to do better, or are they filled with fear that will manifest itself in damaging future performances? Statistically, the second scenario will be the result. Some depends on the child's temperament, which we will discuss later in the chapter. But my point is, how we approach our athletes, the words we use and the actions we take, will impact their mental game to varying degrees.

To get started, you need to understand your baseline. Get real about your parenting style: What kind of environment do you provide for your child currently? Are you the parent who sits in the stands and watches without judgment, or are you feverishly logging your child's statistics and critiquing them and the other players? Are you dictatorial and unwavering in your expectations or do you not attend games at all? Each of those actions represents a different parenting style. Below we will help you define your own parenting style and what the ramifications might have on your athlete. As you continue reading, remember that how you are as a parent or coach directly impacts how your athlete adapts, learns, and grows.

Obviously, all parents, coaches, and children are unique and their interactions with each other are not always easily categorized. As you read through the parenting style descriptions below, do not feel pigeonholed, stereotyped, or guilty. Our intent is to bring light to characteristics you display and assist you in understanding how they may impede or help. Knowing potential obstacles or advantages will help you alter any and all approaches in guiding your athlete. Be honest with yourself, for maximum benefits.

If you are a coach, you can equate the parenting styles we discuss to your coaching style—they go hand in hand—and use this information to inspire children who are not your own too.

Four Types of Parenting Styles

Research has shown that there are four basic overall parenting styles: authoritative, permissive, authoritarian, and neglectful. Each parent is different. Most show characteristics of more than one of these styles, yet when you look at the big picture, one style generally dominates (Mgbemere & Telles, 2013).

The authoritative parent is the optimal parent, the most balanced of the four parenting styles. This parent breeds a healthy environment of structure, open communication, and love. They are warm and always in control of the situation, including with their own emotions. In authoritative parenting, there is a high level of expectations and respect from parent to child and vice-versa. This provides boundaries with room to learn independence. Children raised using an authoritative parenting style tend to be the most well-adjusted children socially (Mgbemere & Telles, 2013).

Before you start claiming, "Oh that's me. I'm definitely this type of parent," answer the following questions:

- Do my children have a structured day?
- Are there set bedtimes or house rules that they must abide by?
- Are there consequences to breaking established rules and do I follow through on them?
- Do I place reasonable expectations on my child, and do they understand them?
- Can my child come to me freely to ask or tell me whatever they want to (Mgbemere & Telles, 2013)?

I will repeat this many times, *be honest with yourself.* The only way effective and meaningful change will happen for you and your athlete will be if you are honest. Think before you answer the previous questions completely. Note, "yes" answers are indicative of an authoritative parent. Know that your answers to these questions are not a "diagnosis" but an indicator for you to understand where your parenting style falls. Again, it may embody aspects of more than one style but go with the style you most identify with.

Next, the permissive parent is one who generally tries to be friends with their child (Mgbemere & Telles, 2013). Although they are typically extremely loving, oftentimes, their rules are light to non-existent or not met with consequences if broken. This parenting style can lead to destructive behaviors in teens because they have little to no rules to guide their decisions. Here are some questions to determine if you are a permissive parent:

- Do you avoid conflict with your child?
- Do you indulge their whims and try to be their friend instead of their parent?
- Do you use bribes to control behavior?

Research suggests that children raised with a permissive parenting style (indicated by "yes" answers to above questions) have low expectations of themselves because their parents place little to no expectations on them. They are low achievers who struggle with decision-making. Often, they can be quite aggressive in nature, perhaps in an effort to seek out rules or the structure their lives lack. Don't be fooled: Kids say they hate structure and rules, but they thrive in their existence and thirst for them when not present. Having no limits opens up a world of possibilities for delinquency, poor grades, drug and alcohol abuse, and other negative behaviors (Mgbemere & Telles, 2013).

The authoritarian parenting style is a "my way or the highway" kind of parent. Authoritarian parents (not to be confused with authoritative parents) are typically strict, unbending, and rarely employ empathy when it comes to their children (Mgbemere & Telles, 2013). As you will see in later chapters, this type of parent will have a difficult time seeing life through their child's eyes, which is critical to their success at some junctures. The authoritarian parent indicators are "yes" answers to these questions:

- Do you enforce strict rules?
- Do you give your child minimal if any choices in their lives?
- Do you make all important decisions for your child?
- Is punishment also a means of coercing your child to do what you want?

Authoritarian parenting is more on par with being a drill sergeant than a loving parent. Control and obedience define the home environment, and oftentimes the children are involved in negative behavior such as bullying. They tend to lash out to combat the tight control their parents have on them. Structure and rules are good but when they're too much, the room for fostering independence is null and void (Mgbemere & Telles, 2013).

A neglectful parenting style means that the parent barely exists. Neglectful parents don't involve themselves in their child's lives and only slightly address their basic needs (Mgbemere & Telles, 2013). Children of neglectful parents rarely receive love or attention from them. Ask yourself these questions. "No" answers for the first three questions and a "yes" for last question will be a sign of being a neglectful parent:

- Do you provide for your child's basic needs?
- Do you know your child's friends and teachers?
- Do you have a good sense of who your child is? What they like? Who they spend time with?
- Is your child alone most of the time?

Neglectful parents make no demands on their children but unlike the permissive parent, the neglectful parent does not provide a warm and loving environment. They aren't trying to be their child's friend; they are simply indifferent altogether. This leaves the child emotionally withdrawn, independent but fearful, and anxiety ridden. These offspring tend to fall into substance abuse more easily than those of other parenting styles (Mgbemere & Telles, 2013).

By virtue of the fact you have this book in your hands, I assume you are interested in guiding your child. I believe I can safely say that you are neither the neglectful parent nor the permissive parent. You may have some permissive tendencies, but overall l am sure you fall into one of the other categories.

Clearly the preferred parenting style for raising emotionally healthy children is the authoritative style, so if that is you, then you are off to a solid start. However, if you think you are more authoritarian, all is not lost. You can alter your parenting style. As with anything, once you acknowledge what your hurdle is, half the battle is won—it just means you have some work to do.

Now some of you may be thinking: *I am X type of parent, but I have more than one child and they each react differently to me when I try and teach them something.* You are correct. Different kids will react differently to your parenting style. Fear not. The other half of the equation of parental influence is your child's temperament, which we will discuss next.

Your Child's Temperament

The clock is ticking. You do a mental analysis of your afternoon itinerary as your youngest yells from the couch while folding his arms in defiance, "I'm not going to baseball practice today!" You force the issue and gain compliance while inwardly contemplating, *Am I doing the right thing? Am I being 'that parent,' forcing my child to participate in a sport?* Yet, inwardly you know that when your child gets to the field, they are engaged and smiling. You relax and assure yourself that nudging him along was a good thing. Meanwhile your oldest child eyes her watch so she won't be late to her practice. Not only did she pack all her own equipment, but she reminds you of the importance of being early to practice about every five minutes. That's when you shake your head and ask yourself, *How did the same parents create two very different individuals?*

Dr. Nick

As a psychologist who has spent the greater part of his career working with children and their parents, I often hear parents declare, "My kids are so different and yet they were raised in the same home with the same rules! How is that possible?" Well, just as two snowflakes are not alike, so too with humans. This inevitably brings about the discussion of nature vs. nurture.

Inherently we are all born with certain characteristics. According to the work of former New York University School of Medicine professors, Alexander Thomas, M.D., and Stella Chess, M.D., there are essentially nine identifiable characteristics which define one's temperament ("New York Longitudinal Study", n.d.). And if you take the nine characteristics that a child is born with (nature) and couple them with all the ways to parent (nurture), then the combinations of humans becomes voluminous, creating vastly different personalities, even within a single-family unit.

What Is Temperament?

Temperament is defined as the factors that make a human uniquely them. Professors Thomas and Chess did a study in 1956 called, "New York Longitudinal Study," in which they defined the nine characteristics of temperament. For it, Thomas and Chess studied children across cultural and economic lines ("New York Longitudinal Study", n.d.).

The nine characteristics of temperament are as follows:

- Sensory threshold: the level of stimulation needed to induce a response
- Activity level: how much motor activity a child has during sleep and wakefulness
- Intensity: how expressive a child is of anger, happiness, sadness, and other emotions
- Rhythmicity: the predictability of the child's bodily functions
- Adaptability: a child's ability to adjust to change
- Mood: their overall disposition
- Approach: a child's reaction to new places or situations
- Persistence: a child's ability to handle challenges

• Distractibility: their ease of distraction or ability to focus

Based upon these nine measurements of a child's temperament, Thomas and Chess concluded that temperaments can be classified into three basic categories: "easy," "slow-to-warm-up," and "difficult." They found that the majority of children in their study fell into one of these three types ("New York Longitudinal Study", n.d.).

Defining Your Child's Temperamental Type

Let's take a close look at the three types of children Thomas and Chess describe in their longitudinal study: The "easy child," "the slow-to-warm-up child," and "the difficult child" ("New York Longitudinal Study", n.d.).

The "easy" child is the child who eats without fuss and has regular sleep cycles. They are adaptable, have an overall positive mood, and go along with what they are taught. Often, the only time these children appear to have difficulty is when they are asked to go against what they learned at home.

The "difficult" child is a 180-degree turn from the "easy" child. The "difficult" child does not adapt well to new things and is usually very negative. It takes time for these children to adjust to changes. Where the "easy" child eats and sleeps without issue, the "difficult" child is inconsistent. They are also prone to tantrums and emotional meltdowns when frustrated. If they are pushed into doing something that is foreign to them, they will exhibit loud, disruptive, and potentially physically aggressive behavior.

The "slow-to-warm-up" child lies somewhere in the middle, as they are moderate across the board. They are the cautious child. These children are typically interested in new things and display moderate levels of activity and intensity. They will warm up to new situations and changes but at a pace that suits them. Although these children are not as easily adaptable as an "easy" child is, with encouragement, they will accept change.

"Slow-to-warm-up" children are extremely sensitive to their emotions, other's emotions, and any other external stimuli. They are easily upset by loud noises, new textures, pain, crowds, and disorganized situations. These children are often labeled as shy, introverted, immature, fearful, or anxious. However, they look before they leap and typically, once they build up trust with individuals, they are quite loyal, open, and outgoing. Their empathetic ways make them loyal individuals who establish strong, close friendships ("New York Longitudinal Study", n.d.).

Temperament can both negatively and positively affect a child's performance and experience with sports. The "easy" child will be more open to learning and typically will not crumble easily if they fail; they will be open to suggestions, making their performance and experience more positive. The "slow-to-warm-up" child may be resistant initially but will become more adaptable and engaged with their sport over time. For the "slow-to-warm-up" child, it's about developing trust. Whereas, those with "difficult" temperaments will be more resistant to change, and any negativity will be hard for them to accept. If the "difficult" child does not perform well, they will be less apt to find the inspiration to do better, ultimately limiting their performance.

It is important to understand that a child's temperament is not cast in stone. Although temperament has been shown to be consistent over time, family environment and life experiences can make a difference. For example, a parent's ability to recognize their child's temperament and note their inherent strengths and weaknesses can create an environment conducive to inspiring strong performance in all areas of their lives. So, it's not solely nature vs. nurture but a combination of both.

Why Is Understanding Temperament Important?

Understanding a child's temperament is important in improving a child's mental game and optimizing their performance. As with any solid plan, you need to understand the facts before you can implement changes. Would you move to another state before understanding why you were leaving, where you wanted to go, and how you would get there? Of course not. So, of course, you would start trying to introduce attributes to a child only after you understood the most effective way it would be received. This is where knowing their temperament comes in.

Understanding all the things that make your athlete who they are is essential to how you will use all the tools we give you in this book. Remember, we want you to enhance your child's mental game and maximize the benefits in other ways as well. The advice in this book, although discussed in relation to sports, transcends into every area of a human's life: social, academic, and spiritual.

I caution you however; once you define your child's temperament, do not label them as such. That information is good to know for reactionary and pro-active parenting responses but saying them out loud could potentially harm your child.

Correlation Between Environment and Temperament

How your child interacts and emotionally deals with their world directly impacts how they perceive or absorb critical information—specifically, information from you. Once you know your child's temperament and your parenting style, you can more accurately determine how to make it an effective mix, if not present already.

It is the mix or the "goodness of fit" between your child's temperament and their environment that matters most. The match or mismatch between a child's temperament and their environment determines the productive growth of the child. Children are more likely to perform at their highest level in sports and beyond when there is goodness of fit. "Goodness of fit" is often achieved when their temperaments are valued and their personalities are supported ("Goodness of Fit", n.d.). For instance, healthy social and personality development takes place when there is compatibility between the child and the demands and expectations of you, the parent. When "goodness of fit" is poor, temperament is often not respected nor accommodated and may result in the athlete being less receptive to any parental guidance (Sanson, Hemphill and Smart, 2004).

Stepping back and observing their child's temperament can help parents become aware of individual differences, understand how temperament may be related to their child's behaviors, and develop strategies to increase the goodness of fit between the child and their environment. However, it is important for parents to understand that there are no "good" or "bad" temperament traits only unique ways in which we express ourselves or respond to the world. Given your child's temperament, here are some parental tips and strategies to use that will help them reach their full potential.

Advice for parents of the "difficult" child (Rajaratnam and Gracias, n.d.):

1. Understand the reasons: Your child's behavior is a manifestation of their innate temperament. So, remember that they don't behave in a particular manner intentionally. As a parent, try to understand the root cause of their behavior. For example, what were the events leading up to a specific reaction? Then focus on helping your child learn how to tackle the challenges. At the same time, reinforce positive behavior.

2. Be patient: Dealing with a "difficult" child is challenging and requires a great deal of patience and effort. Empathize with his or her feelings in difficult situations and react calmly instead of getting worked up.

3. Maintain a schedule: Because your child finds it difficult to adjust to routines, it is important to maintain structure. Keep predictable schedules for sleeping and waking up, mealtimes, and other routine tasks. Let your child know in advance about any impending changes in the schedule to help them be prepared. And avoid cramming too many activities into a day, as too much activity can be stressful and overwhelming for a "difficult" child.

4. Have realistic expectations: Your expectations should always be age appropriate. Discipline your child by clearly explaining the limits and consequences and avoid overreacting. Getting agitated when your child throws a tantrum will only induce a power struggle between the two of you.

Advice for parents of the "slow-to-warm-up" child:

1. Accept the trait: Even though your child warms slowly, avoid labeling them as shy or reserved, and don't compare them with their peers or siblings in the hope of making them act differently. Focus on their strengths and nurture them patiently.

2. Prepare your child: Your child may feel unsure and take time to adapt to many new experiences. So, prepare them in advance for what is going to

happen. For example, let them know what's going to happen ahead of time. Encourage them to express their feelings about the change. Don't attempt to push them into the spotlight, as this could scare them and make them feel hesitant rather than confident.

3. Be responsive: Your child will, most likely, be reluctant to take part in new activities or interact with unfamiliar individuals. You can help them overcome fears or unwillingness to reach out to others by giving the right assurances without being over-protective. In time, a "slow-to-warm-up" child will usually grow up to be more outgoing.

Advice for parenting the "easy" child:

1. Stay attentive: Raising a child with an easy temperament is relatively effortless as they usually adapt well to different situations. However, parents of an easy child often make the mistake of taking them for granted and not giving them due attention. Make the effort to stay involved (Rajaratnam and Gracias, n.d.).

2. Check in: Randomly check to be sure there are no concerns or issues your "easy" child would like to share. It's important that they know you are listening and that they can come to you with any problems.

While all these parenting suggestions will help increase you and your child's "goodness of fit," it's important to note that maybe the most important parenting advice when addressing your child's temperament is to assess your own temperament (Thomas and Chess, 1997).

Exploring your child's temperament in relation to yours may provide valuable information about how the child is responding to the environment around them (Thomas and Chess, 1997). For example, if your child tends to take his time when changing from one activity to the next and you quickly sign him up for a new sport without giving the child notice, the child may demonstrate resistance to the new sport. However, if you give sufficient notice, the child may transition to new activities happily. Understanding both temperaments will help you to find the best approach for the emotional, social, and learning needs of the child (Bates et al, 2012). This newfound understanding allows for increased harmony between parent and child, ultimately allowing for the child to grow and reach their maximum potential (Bates et al, 2012).

After reading this chapter, I hope you now have a better idea how the environment you create for your child and their temperament style intersect (Thomas and Chess, 1997). Understand you are the adult, and therefore it is your job to make sure you are valuing and supporting their individual temperament style and personality. By doing this, you will see your athlete truly excel. It is also important to note, that in order to see positive improvement in your child's growth and development, you must be consistent and repetitious. As with anything, repetition and consistency are necessary to embedding a change. A parent's understanding and respect for their children's temperaments are vital for their children to thrive and develop (Sanson, Hemphill and Smart, 2004).

CHAPTER 2

Mindset

One of the toughest roles a sport parent has is spectator. Sometimes watching our kids play a sport is so painful, it's on par with getting a root canal or paying taxes. We've all had those moments: you sit down to watch your athlete and the first thing you say to yourself is, "Please let him have a good game" knowing, with dread, the destructive qualities failure can impart.

Things can spiral down fast after the game kicks off. Perhaps your athlete is tending goal and your stomach churns, as if you just downed a dozen hot wings. He misses the first shot and the other team scores. *Just brush it off*, you try to communicate telepathically to your kid. The next shot goes toward the right corner and your goalie moves to the left. Your head drops in your hands.

After the game ends, you walk toward your minivan with a downtrodden athlete in tow, praying his lackluster performance won't derail his motivation to practice or desire to play at all. Pushing through, you bravely ask, "Want to go kick the ball around? You can be in the goal?"

"No, I just want to go home."

Part of you wants to lecture and the other part wants to console. Do you become one of "those parents" berating their 9-year-old as they exit the field? Do you pretend that the whole thing didn't happen? Do you try to cheer them up with ice cream? How do you turn an attitude around and get your player back on track effectively? What are the right words, or should you use no words at all?

Dr. Nick

Would you watch a game if you already knew its outcome? I suspect not. Some of what makes sports exciting is the unknown. But the unknown is also the key source of anxiety for players, parents, and coaches—even for the world's top performers in sports. Anxiety is a basic human emotion, and no one is immune to it. It's why we sit on the edge of our seats when our kids play sports, and why our kids get nervous before a game or competition.

I know young, highly successful athletes who've relayed stories of how they vomit before every game. Despite their abilities, they still have anxiety and fear of the unknown outcome, and vomiting is the way their body physiologically responds to the stress. You may ask: How can an athlete emotionally eliminate any and all anxiety or fear?

I am sorry to tell you, but you can never get rid of anxiety. Eradication of fear will never happen. As we discussed in the previous chapter, you can't change the core of who a child is, but you can change their secondary responses. Specifically, you can't eliminate your athlete's anxiety, but you can alter how they respond to it emotionally, and thereby, positively impact their performance. Altering how they respond to stress entails fostering mental attributes we will discuss throughout the book. In this chapter, we will focus on mindset.

Anxiety is present for everyone in sport to varying degrees. Typically, the more resources an athlete has, the better equipped they are to respond to feelings of anxiety or fear. By "resources" I am referring to the physical preparedness and emotional and/or mental attributes a player has, such as mindset, which we will explain in this chapter, or grit and self-efficacy, which we will discuss in later chapters. The player's history of physical performance coupled with strong mental and emotional attributes will help the player reduce any potential fear or anxiety that could negatively impact their performance.

Who do you think has higher anxiety in competition: an athlete who has years of experience or the athlete who is just emerging? Typically, of course, it would be the latter, but the fact remains, both will possess some amount of anxiety. Again, the more the athlete has to draw from (their resources), the less anxiety will be produced. One of the most important resources an athlete has is mindset.

What Is Mindset?

Stanford University professor and author Carol Dweck brilliantly explains the term mindset in her book by the same name. Mindset is one's perceptions, beliefs, or attitudes (Dweck, 2006). Although there are many different beliefs and attitudes out there, Dweck says any one person's mindset can be categorized into two distinct categories: fixed and growth.

A fixed mindset is a focus solely on outcome. In sports, a person with a fixed mindset believes that a positive outcome derives solely from winning. To that person, falling short of winning equates to failure and is something to fear, not something you use to learn from.

A growth mindset is a belief that, although outcome is important, the focus is on growth, learning, and improving as the immediate goals. The growth-minded person receives as much excitement from the challenge and the pursuit as they do from the win. Should the growth-minded individual fail, they do not see themselves as a failure, but rather they take the opportunity to define areas of improvement, enabling success in the future. They embrace the idea that life is a marathon and not a relay race (Dweck, 2006).

Fixed and Growth Mindsets

"All I wanted was a chance" – Isaiah Thomas

Consider Isaiah Thomas, who in 2011 abandoned his thriving college basketball career—a year early—to follow his dream to play in the NBA. His 5-foot 9-inch stature presented some risks in the NBA, where the average height of a player is a staggering 6-foot 7-inches. Yet, the risk paid off. Isaiah made the 2011 NBA draft as the last pick of that year (Spears, 2017).

Ask yourself: if you were Thomas, almost a foot shorter than the average professional basketball player, and the last guy picked for the season, how much anxiety would you carry? How would you feel going into the start of the season? Perhaps, you'd be intimidated, and a smidge worried about measuring up. Again, an unknown outcome will weigh heavy on the player's mind.

I suspect Thomas had some amount of trepidation, but it clearly didn't impact his ability to perform. In fact, he went on to become a two-time, all-star NBA player in 2016 and 2017, among many other accolades. What separates him from most people? Why was he not paralyzed by fear? Isaiah displays many attributes of a champion, and we will explore those throughout this book, but one of the most critical attributes he possesses is his mindset.

As a new draftee in 2011, Thomas saw opportunity. Where many might perceive his height as being a negative, Thomas didn't dwell on what he didn't have that the other players did. Instead of seeing the fact that he was the last player drafted as a negative, Thomas focused on the fact that he achieved his initial goal (Spears, 2017). His mindset saw an open door and he walked through it without question. His focus was not on the cards stacked against him, but rather the cards in his favor: he was drafted into the NBA and thus given the opportunity to grow, learn, and develop as a basketball player. This exemplifies a growth-minded athlete.

Let's also look at Shaun White, an Olympic Gold Medalist in snowboarding. In 2017, while training to qualify for the 2018 Olympics, White pushed himself to learn the double cork 1440 or YOLO flip (Roenigk, 2018). During an attempt at the 1440, he crashed, slamming his face into the side of the half-pipe. Despite needing 62 stitches and spending five days in intensive care, and the fact that his family wanted him to quit, White made the decision to go back out on the snow. "Stepping out on the snow again means I am willing to let this happen to myself again," White said in an interview with ABC news. "That's a big decision."

After recovering, White went to the 2017 X-Games in Colorado to qualify for the 2018 Olympics. On his final run, an anxious White knew if he failed to deliver a solid performance, he could lose his chance at his third Olympic gold medal in the men's half-pipe—the one that eluded him in the 2014 Olympics in Sochi. Despite his anxiety, he scored a mind-blowing 100, a perfect score, and ultimately made the 2018 Olympic team.

At the 2018 Olympics, after falling during a previous run, White had one last chance to reach that third gold. Knowing he had to put it all out there or go home without reaching his goal, White performed a perfect front-side double cork 1440—the move that had put him in the hospital—and a cab double cork 1440 combo. He never tried this in practice at all, but the performance won him his coveted third Olympic gold medal in the men's half-pipe. After the win, his father relayed his feelings in an interview, "Seeing him cry made me cry. My tears are joy. It's all over. All that pressure he's had since Sochi [the 2014 Olympics where he missed the third gold], it built a fire under him" (Roenigk, 2018).

What got White past his anxiety to earn that perfect score in the X-Games and in the final run in the 2018 Olympics? He certainly had his moments of failure—failures that would sideline even the best competitors and fill them with anxiety. So, what made him get back up and decide to face any anxiety or fears and push himself beyond his limits? It was White's mindset.

A growth-minded White came back from a fear-producing fall and went on to achieve his goal in the Olympics. He admitted that his anxiety and fear were very present. What reduced those negative emotions was the opportunity to be better and achieve his goal.

To add to your understanding of what growth and fixed mindsets look like, let's take a look at this story: A ten-year old boy was at his weekly baseball game. His team was losing with no room to recover. As one of his teammates displayed angst over the situation, the young man consoled, "We're just here to have fun."

Immediately, their coach reprimanded, "Don't ever let me hear you say those words again! We're here to win!"

Unbelievable for ten-year old recreational baseball maybe, but a true story, nonetheless.

Shortly after hearing that story, I watched the television coverage of the first round of a major golf tournament. As one high-profile player entered the clubhouse, a reporter asked if he was disappointed with his place on the leaderboard. This player was in third place after completing the day's round, under par, and in horrific weather conditions. The player smiled and answered, quite matter-of-factly, that he was proud of how he played given the weather. The player acknowledged his few mistakes, but said he learned from them and planned to hit it hard again the next day.

What is different between the coach and the pro golfer? The simple answer: mindset. The pro golfer, like Shaun White and Isaiah Thomas, displayed the same growth mindset. The coach in the first story, however, had a fixed mindset. He focused solely on the end result that day. He asserted no value in fun or playing to learn, solely in playing to win. Instead, he chose anger and admonishment to instill fear as a motivator, leaving the boys with those words lingering in their young minds that day. The potential harm of those words could range from minimal to severe depending on the child, but either way, none of the players learned valuable lessons to take with them into the next game. Using fear and negativity didn't teach these young players where they made mistakes and how to correct them going forward.

Fear never works as a motivator long term. It's insidious and grows like a fungus in the mind. If the player never learns how to respond to that fear, it will eventually diminish any physical performance.

In the fixed mindset, validation is solely found through winning. When an athlete with a fixed mindset fails, they immediately perceive themselves as a failure. This damage can, at its most impactful, be debilitating. One with a fixed mindset could never envision a loss as part of the path to learning, growing, and achieving greatness. Far too often, a person with this mindset never achieves their real potential because they are afraid to push themselves to grow and learn. They think: *What if I push and then I fail again* (Dweck, 2006)?

Our second story—of the pro golfer—demonstrates a growth-minded attitude. The pro golfer wasn't upset with his placement on the leaderboard. He chose to focus on his game and how he would handle things the next day. The knowledge he acquired from the mistakes he made that day would help him correct them in the following days of competition.

Let's look at it another way: When babies learn to walk, they fall constantly. Yet, babies don't fear falling. They get back up and keep trying. Each new day brings improvement in their skills and eventually they achieve their objective. That's what it means to be growth minded. Can you imagine if, as a baby, you were encumbered with the same fears as many adults? Think about that for a second. Learning to walk would take on a new meaning entirely.

Someone with a growth mindset focuses on the process and sees life as a continuous path of learning and growing (Dweck, 2006). Growth-minded individuals see winning as a byproduct of their hard work and determination. These individuals receive validation not just in the win, but in the process of growing, learning, and improving.

Now, obviously, fixed minded people don't always fail. When do fixed minded people succeed? According to Dweck, fixed-minded people thrive, "when things are safely within their grasp. When things get too challenging, when they're not feeling smart or talented, they lose interest-" (Dweck, 2006).

For example, if an athlete has a fixed mindset, they prefer to compete in situations that are a "sure win." In new or more challenging situations, a fixed-minded athlete's anxiety heightens to such potentially crippling levels that they often fall short of winning. And, instead of learning from that experience and growing as a player, they will feel defeated and will avoid that challenge again.

One of my clients, a competitive junior golfer, had the opportunity to play in a higher age bracket. His skills as a player more than warranted it. However, when presented with that decision, he chose to play in the lower age bracket. That put him at the top of the playing field and yes, he racked in multiple wins that season. The next season, because of his age, the choice was made for him. He did not face the same success level, and he ended that season feeling depleted and contemplating if he should stay in the game at all.

Conversely, given a challenging situation, a growth-minded athlete would attack the obstacle with a focus on pushing themselves and developing as a player just like Shaun White and Isaiah Thomas did. Growth and improving their abilities are at the forefront of their thoughts.

I have seen this with many of my clients who, unlike the aforementioned golfer, decide to play in the higher brackets to focus on learning from the better players. They see it as an opportunity to grow and they believe that the wins will eventually come as a matter of course.

Armed with this knowledge, analyze yourself and your child. Ask yourself: Am I of a fixed mindset or a growth mindset? Is my child of a fixed mindset or a growth mindset? Let's look at some questions to help you determine this.

In the book *Mindset*, Dweck (2016) asks the reader to read each statement below and answer if you:

Mostly agree with it or disagree with it.

1. Your intelligence is something very basic about you that you can't change very much.
2. You can learn new things, but you can't really change how intelligent you are.
3. No matter how much intelligence you have, you can always change quite a bit.
4. You can always substantially change how intelligent you are.

Questions 1 and 2 are fixed mindset questions. Questions 3 and 4 reflect a growth mindset. If you agree more with 1 and 2 then you have a fixed mindset about your abilities and if you agree more with 3 and 4, then obviously you tend toward a growth mindset. (Dweck, 2006)

You can have a fixed mindset in one area of your life and a growth mindset in others (Dweck, 2016). You could, for example, make mistakes as a spouse and accept your failings as learning opportunities to becoming a better husband or wife. Yet, while at work, you could be a very fixed minded person. You may believe that you could only achieve a successful career if you don't make any mistakes, if you only take on work you know you can excel in, or if you fear challenges. The first step is to recognize where in your life you have these limiting beliefs and where your child has them, assuming they are present at all.

If you, your child, or both of you have fixed mindsets, you may be wondering: *Are we doomed?* Absolutely not. Mindsets can be altered to produce optimal results for you and your athlete. We will discuss how to make those changes later in the chapter.

Natural vs. Effort

I've known many who hold the theory: If you have to work at something then you really aren't that talented. They believe athletes are born not made. These are beliefs of a fixed-minded individual. And often these thoughts limit these individuals from ever reaching their full potential.

The fixed mindset puts stock in the naturally talented, gifted, and prodigal (Dweck, 2016). People with this mindset see "naturals" as people who should be revered and emulated. They put little stock in individuals who put effort into their sport. Carol Dweck states that those with fixed mindsets believe "effort can reduce you-" (Dweck, 2006). They believe you are somehow less of a winner if you have to work at your talent, and therefore your true talent or abilities should be doubted (Dweck, 2006).

But, the growth-minded individual sees effort as necessary to propel themselves to greater achievements. Growth-minded athletes truly love what they do, enjoy the path to greatness, and focus on constantly pushing themselves. These individuals are all about the challenge. Winning and success become the reward of what they do and who they are.

I know a young athlete whose coach complained he didn't practice effectively and never put in the time he should. "If he put more effort into developing his already exemplary skills, he would go so much further," his coach lamented.

So, I asked this athlete, "Why don't you practice more and do specific drills your coach gives you?"

"If I have to put that much effort into it, then I'm not that talented." This athlete clearly made a correlation between winning and talent, not between winning and effort. He went on the say, "There are kids who play so much better than me. They're just naturally good players." This player felt defeated by another's innate or perceived talent, and he failed to find inspiration in it. He saw limitations instead of growth opportunities, where with hard work and determination, he might grow and potentially surpass the other "more talented" players. He put zero value in effort and placed blame on lack of talent. Was his thought process correct? No, not if he ever wanted to improve. The sad truth of this story: his mindset was failing him. His abilities were not.

Many of us have heard the story of Michael Jordan. For all of Michael Jordon's success in basketball, it didn't come easy for him. He wasn't a "natural." He didn't even make his high school varsity team ("Newsweek", 2015). After not seeing his name on the team roster, did Jordan give up? Did he believe his failure to make the team defined him as "no good" at basketball? In a 2015 *Newsweek* article, Jordan stated, that initially the cut hurt, and he went home and cried ("Newsweek", 2015). This moment was fleeting, and he soon found his motivation. The motivation, he admitted, was fueled by his failing to make the team roaster. He chose to practice and work harder at his skills instead of sitting home licking his wounds over not being a "natural." "Whenever I was working out and got tired and figured I ought to stop, I'd close my eyes and see that list in the locker room without my name on it," Jordan stated, "That usually got me going again-" ("Newsweek", 2015).

In 1979, the following year, Jordan made the varsity team ("Newsweek", 2015). His growth mindset pushed him to take on the challenge and he achieved the success he desired. Clearly, that mindset set him on a pathway toward success in the future as a professional basketball player.

Character's Impact on Mindset

What is the most important trait that separates the fixed mindset from the growth mindset? The simple answer: character. In her book, Carol Dweck (2006) defines character as "the ability to dig down and find strength to persevere even when things are going against you." As Dweck points out, there is a one-to-one correlation between character and a growth mindset—one doesn't exist without the other. The growth mindset focuses on the process, not the immediate outcome. The growth-minded individual isn't playing a sport solely to win every event, but to learn and excel over time. Character is what propels the growth-minded athlete to persevere despite setbacks (Dweck, 2016).

No matter the sport, age, or level, an athlete facing difficulty or challenges, either physical or emotional, has two choices: give up or push through. How many times have we watched an athlete endure difficulty and still finish well, if not on top, while another struggles and gives up? How many times have you asked: *What makes one athlete succumb and another persevere?* Mindset clearly plays a role, and one of the key factors to a growth mindset is the existence of character.

It's important to understand that character is both enhanced by sports and necessary for excellence in sports. Character reflects in this instance the ability to keep going when everything is going wrong. In competition, the athlete who pushes themselves despite adversity—no matter how challenging or how defeated that athlete feels—is the individual who will eventually achieve excellence. To foster this trait in their athletes, parents must demonstrate the right way to handle themselves in their own times of adversity.

Let's look at this from a parent's perspective. There are degrees of stress and anxiety when your athlete shows up, but their game doesn't. Seeing your athlete struggle, either emotionally or physically, is both difficult and challenging. The stress and anxiety can originate from hearing other parents' comments, watching a coach reprimand or push, seeing physical or emotional hurt in their athlete, and sometimes fighting the desire to try and "fix" the problem for them. Let's face it: sports are stressful for both the athlete and the parents. This is critical to understand because, again, parents are the biggest influencers of an athlete's environment. How parents act in the face of challenge directly impacts an athlete's development of character.

Let's revisit the Shaun White story. Before the 2018 Olympics when White took that incredible fall, his parents were halfway around the world (Roenigk, 2018). One can only imagine the stress and anxiety they felt at that time. His mother was quoted by ABC News as saying, "I wanted him to stop snowboarding-" (Roenigk, 2018). Yet, despite the concern of loved ones, White made the choice to get back on that half-pipe in the X-Games to qualify for the Olympics.

In that same interview, White's mother goes on to say, "We never doubted him. We were just afraid-" (Roenigk, 2018). When White made it to the Olympics, his parents were with him and supporting him all the way. They had their concerns and expressed them—even White had his fears— but they supported his decision, nonetheless. They demonstrated their character to push through, even under the most stressful situation. This is a clear example of parent and athlete pushing through, of both having the character to take on the task ahead, despite any and all obstacles, including fear.

Let's look at this from another angle. My client, a junior golfer, had been conditioned by his own father to believe that if he didn't do well on a series of holes, he'd be giving the game away. This theory was so ingrained in his mindset that time and time again, he threw in the towel when he had a series of bad holes. The thought of scrambling or "grinding it out" to get a better score never became an option for him—he determined the ending before the end. The parent's fixed mindset instilled a fixed mindset in his child.

Whereas the fixed mindset athlete sees that he's losing and gives up, the athlete with a growth mindset sees his struggle as a motivator to push on. No matter how hard the challenge or how defeated the player feels, the growth-minded player cranks it out, pushing himself. That is *character*.

Again, what kind of mindset do you and your child have? Do each of you look at each challenge as an opportunity to grow, or do you fear the challenge will set you up for failure? Assess both you and your child exclusively. Hold your observations in your head as we move on in the chapter.

How to Become Growth Minded

What is the one thing a professional athlete and a junior athlete have in common? They both practice basic skills, all the time. Why? Because the basic skills can never be mastered. Nothing is 100% a 100% of the time: that's just part of being human. So, before we discuss how to become growth minded, you and your athlete must understand this premise: basic skills will never be mastered. A player will always be practicing basic skills to improve their game. This is not unlike the statement I made about never fully getting rid of anxiety, stress, or fear—eradication is not possible. Instead, practice altering your responses to minimizing the anxiety, stress, or fear.

Now, whether you desire to change yourself, your athlete, or both from a fixed mindset to a growth mindset, practicing basic skills will go from a finite objective to an infinite process. The objective of the growth-minded athlete is to constantly improve their skill set both physically and mentally. This is how they build the "resources" we talked about earlier. The more "resources" they have, the better they'll respond to anxiety or stress and hence, the better they'll perform. A growth-minded individual holds this as a standard truth on which they practice, compete, and obtain their goals.

You may ask: *If the goal is to change an athlete's mindset from fixed to growth, why do parents or coaches need to be growth minded? Isn't this about the athlete?* Well, how our athletes perceive themselves often is a reflection of how they think we see them. We need to be careful of the messages we send to our athletes through our actions and words if we want them to get the most out of sports. We need to "walk the talk" or "practice what we preach".

Now let's suppose you, your child, or both of you have fixed mindsets. How do you change, if your entire life you were led to believe you should focus on the good grades or on winning, and if you couldn't do it, then you were a big, fat failure? How do you change years of believing one thing? The answer: patience and persistence.

Change rarely happens overnight, it takes time and repetition to change one's mindset. Like a muscle in the body, the brain needs repetition for something to become automatic or learned. When a golfer needs to make changes to his or her swing, do they make the change and then it works? No, it takes considerable repetition over time before that new swing becomes a learned skill. The same is true for most new skills we learn, especially when working with a player's mental game.

Often, I have new clients who come to see me and expect that I will "cure" their fears in an hour-long session. It's not that simple. The process to change any ingrained belief or habit takes time and repetition to become a new belief. Becoming a growth-minded individual is no exception to this rule.

Patience is also key in changing one's mindset—patience with yourself and your child as you move through this process. You will stumble from time to time: forgive and move on. Trust you have it in you and that your child has the ability to adopt the new mindset. Set forth with persistence and you will succeed.

Where do you start? I am going to make an assertion that will make a person with a fixed mindset cringe: In life, failure is inevitable. At some point or points, a person will fail. Should a person accept it and move on? No, don't accept it, but find motivation in it. Make it the driver for growth and learning.

Growth-minded people by no means love to fail. They do, however, look at failure more closely to find the benefit in it. They go through their mistakes step by step until they find that teachable moment that will make them better. When you or your athlete fails, you need to stop and find the learning moment in it. Ask yourself or the athlete: Where was the mistake or error, and how should it be different? What does the athlete need to focus on in practice going forward?

Note, this discussion requires an honest look at the situation, and leaves no place to play the blame game. It's not a time to blame someone or something else for an athlete's failure to perform at their best.

Failure is not to be feared. Failure is natural. And failure is an essential part of the learning process. Without failure, we won't grow and learn. Think of the way muscles grow. Muscles, when they are exhausted or pushed beyond their limits fail and tear. If you rest the muscle for a day or so, the muscle repairs itself and gets stronger, but only because it failed. If you lift weights, you certainly understand this concept. Weightlifters typically work on one set of muscles at a time. For example, on Monday they may work their legs, Tuesday they may work their abdominals, and Wednesday they may work their arms. This type of routine is designed to rest the muscles after exhaustion and allow for them to repair themselves and grow stronger.

When I speak with my athletes, I always ask them, in relation to their performance, "How do you know how much you have in you?" They will inevitably reply, "I don't know." I say, "Well then, you're not trying hard enough. You need to push yourself to the point where you fail to know your current limits." Some shudder at this thought because they believe *failure* is a word that shouldn't be in their vocabulary. However, let me be very clear: I use the word "failure" in terms of execution, never in terms of winning. If an athlete fails to execute with excellence, then they have learned their current limit. Knowing their limit is crucial for growth. Knowing where they have failed will allow them to set new goals and to grow. Failure is a starting point, not an end point.

For example, take any recruit for a fire or police academy, especially in larger, metropolitan areas. One large part of their day is physical training. For many of the recruits, when they started, they had no idea if they could keep up physically. But, several weeks in, each one of the recruits can tell you what their limits are because training everyday takes them to the point where they can no longer execute the skill with excellence.

In terms of your young athlete, there are many skills they do automatically, depending on their age and ability. And every athlete has some skills they can execute well without issue, such as catching a baseball, making foul shots, or running a mile without stopping. But what about those skills they try but can't execute well? It's at those moments where they push themselves to attempt to execute the skill but fail that limits are established. And by pushing themselves I don't always mean in the sense of stamina or physical exhaustion. It could mean pushing themselves to try a new skill they may have avoided out of fear or self-doubt. For the younger athlete, you will have to guide them in understanding their limits and how to challenge themselves. The older athletes they should know their physicality well enough that they can identify their own limits and know how to challenge themselves.

It should be noted that young athletes should never be pushed to points of exhaustion, either physically or mentally, to test their limits. As their parent or coach, you can help them identify their current limits through analyzing how they execute skills during a practice or a game, for example.

So, how do you change your athlete's view of failure? Again, you need to find the lesson hidden in failure. The athlete needs to be able to dissect their performance honestly and see where they need to make changes, where they need to strengthen their skills, and/or how they should emotionally handle a situation. Whatever the outcome, when an athlete fails, they must walk away with a sense of what they need to do to improve for the next performance. And to do this effectively, the athlete needs to know that they have your support and that your love isn't attached to a win or loss.

The back-up quarterback for the Philadelphia Eagles lead his team to winning the 2018 Super Bowl. When Nick Foles addressed the media, he attributed his Super Bowl success to all his previous failures. He said it was all the times he didn't win, or didn't perform his best, that made him learn and grow as an athlete (Bandini, 2018). If athletes don't push themselves and stretch their limits, they won't fail. Lack of failure stunts growth.

Growth-minded athletes don't fear failure; they fear never growing. Fixed mindsets are stifled by failure. As parents, we need to teach our children how to fail and that effort is essential to developing their skills.

The Impact of Vocabulary

Along with time, repetition, patience, and changing how you address failure, the vocabulary you use must change in order to become growth minded. The internal and external words you use with your athlete need to change. Below are effective guidelines to follow in order to develop a growth mindset:

1. *Focus on growth (Dweck, 2016).* Stop talking about winning or getting top grades and start focusing on growth. Please do not misunderstand: It's not that those things are no longer important. I think we can all agree that getting good grades and winning are the ultimate goals. However, the process to getting there should be focused on the journey, not the destination. If you shift that focus, the end results will be there (Dweck, 2106).

    For example: if your child swims his heart out and comes in second, do you say: "Why didn't you come in first?" No, you say, "I am proud of how you pushed yourself out there, and I see you gave your all. You showed great passion and perseverance. What did you learn from today's meet?"

    Now, let's play devil's advocate and say your child came in second but didn't put in any effort out there. Do you berate the child with tough love sayings like, "Cut the laziness and start performing out there?" You do if you are fixed minded, but if you are growth minded, you might say, "I didn't see a ton of effort today. How do you feel you did? You have to work hard and learn from these events if you want to grow as a swimmer."

2. **Praise effort not accomplishment** *(Dweck, 2016)*. Find the growth factor in failure, not the reduction factor. When you praise the effort, kids will learn to see effort in a positive light, something that's part of the journey toward success. However, if you only praise accomplishments, then what they hear will be that winning is the only thing that matters (Dweck, 2016).

For example, you run off the stands and grab your player and say, "You won the game! Great job buddy!" What your player hears is that you value winning. But, if you were to run off those stands and say, "Good game! I am so proud of how hard you worked out on that field. You made sure to get in front of the ball like your coach showed you in practice. I like the effort!" What you have now done is shown your player that you recognize his hard work, and that his efforts are paying off. You kept the praise specific and focused on player development, not on winning or losing.

3. **Choose your words carefully** (Dweck, 2016). What your kids hear may be different than what you mean, so choose your words carefully. Make sure what you say conveys what you mean, and what they inevitably hear.

Word usage is important when talking with your children whether you are providing praise, as we just discussed, or encouragement. In her book, Carol Dweck suggests changing the term we use from *can* to *how*. For example, stop implying: *Can you do this?* Instead, you should imply: *How will you accomplish this?* Approaching things with the attitude that your athlete can accomplish something, but they need to figure out how, is far better than questioning their outcome off the bat. Starting anything with doubt is like sabotage before they even start (Dweck, 2016).

When your daughter comes to you and says she wants to join the field hockey team, do you ask, "You think you can do that?" or "Do you think you should do that?" Or do you respond, "Ok, I'm proud of you for challenging yourself with something new. How are you going to handle it from here? What are your next steps?"

If you chose one of the two first responses (fixed-minded responses), your daughter thinks, *He doubts I can do it. Maybe he's right and maybe I'll look stupid if I try it.* Now, if you use the last response (growth-minded response), she thinks *He's got my back no matter the outcome and he's just proud of my effort.* Which would you find more inspiring?

4. ***Work to change your athlete's internal monologue*** (Dweck, 2016). Suppose you have that reluctant kid who, no matter how growth-minded your words, won't take that leap and try anything. The child is paralyzed by the idea of failing, or even worse, failing and everyone seeing it. What do you do? First, you stay growth minded. Second, you work on changing the child's mindset. You need to get them to change their internal monologue with themselves. Like Dweck says, for example, change the words they use from *can* to *how*. Again, this takes considerable patience and perseverance on your part but it's crucial for them (Dweck, 2016).

    Suppose your son says he doesn't want to play basketball because in his mind, he's not very good. How should you address this with him? First you listen, then you ask, "Well, when you aren't good at something how should you handle it?"

    He may respond, "I don't know, practice I guess?"

    "Sometimes in life we need to challenge ourselves to grow and succeed. There is just as much fun in playing to learn, as there is in playing to win. I know you will put the effort in and learn so much if you play."

Remember, analyze the situation first, then choose growth-minded words, focusing on effort, challenges, character, and learning from failure. Make sure your athlete understands this mantra: *Success will be the byproduct of the compilation of efforts along the way. Stumbles are just part of the process toward excellence in performance.*

I caution you, do not confuse growth-minded vocabulary to mean: "Only say something positive." The theory of only saying something positive to our children can be as detrimental as a fixed mindset. The goal is not to instill a false sense of self-worth, but to instill growth-minded attitudes by focusing on moving forward and learning. You want your athlete to love challenges and to assess themselves and their performances honestly. Truth is the only way the athlete can improve and learn to achieve excellence.

The truth, however, should never be phrased in such a way that is cruel or hurtful. The truth should focus on specifics and facts but always with a growth-minded tone.

For example: your daughter played her worse tennis match ever. She is devastated. You noticed that she wasn't anticipating the shots like she normally does. How do you address it?

A.) Do you tell her she did fabulously and that it was just bad luck she didn't win? No, it's a lie. It's being positive, but it's a lie and won't help her at all. You spare her self-image, but she won't feel the need to work on where she went wrong.

B.) Do you say, "You sucked out there today. Where is your head?" No, it may be the truth but it's negative and hurtful. Again, nothing gets learned and you'll damage her self-image.

C.) You say, "I noticed you weren't anticipating the shots like you normally do today. How do you feel you did, and where do you think you need to improve? Learn from this match and take that information with you when you practice." This creates an open discussion around facts, without judgment or focus on the fact that she lost. The tone is one of encouragement, not admonishment.

Obviously, option C is the best possible way to handle the situation because it allows the player to drive herself to improve going forward. It nurtures the growth mindset, creating a pathway for future excellence in performance.

Additionally, remember to make sure your player understands that failing at the basic skills of the game is part of the process. Professional athletes also fail at basic skills at times. Basic skills will never be mastered, but you can improve your basic skills through repetition in practice if you keep a growth mindset. It's an important truth all athletes share.

Recently, a friend shared a story with me about her youngest son, Jack. Back in the third grade, when Jack started playing lacrosse, she loved watching him go to practice and learn the basics. But by the fourth grade, his team was playing teams from other towns and obviously the expectations on the players were higher.

When the coach asked if anyone wanted to try the goalie position, Jack thought about it, telling his mother he would try at the next game. Her fears ate away at her. She worried he would fail miserably and that he'd be treated poorly by the other players for allowing goals. She knew how competitive the parents were and saw that it was beginning to trickle down to the kids.

Driving to the next game, the boy declared, "Today, I'm going to ask to play goalie!"

"No, don't ask to be goalie!" she said, as she pulled the car up to the field.

"Why?"

"I think you should wait on it. I'm not sure you'd like it." She stammered searching for a way to steer him clear of a potential confidence buster moment. But, before she knew it, Jack was out of the car and heading toward the field.

A sea of helmets and uniforms took to the field as the mom arrived at the bleachers and sat down. Another parent leaned over and asked, "Hey, isn't that Jack in the goal?"

The mom nearly passed out. She stood up and ran down the bleachers to stand on the sidelines in complete fear. During the game, the other team barely got the ball to the goal and when they did, Jack caught each one. He smiled coming off the field, running over to his mother.

"Jack, I thought you heard me and weren't going to ask to be goalie."

"Yeah, but I wanted to try it. I liked it. Coach says I'm in for the next game! Isn't that great?"

The mom smiled. "Yes, it is."

Jack heard his mother's pleas, but his mind was open and growth oriented. The mom's fixed mindset was what made her worried about him failing and feeling awful about himself. His growth mindset said he wanted to try and push himself and maybe find a position on the team he liked better. He was right on all points.

Stop protecting your athletes from trying things at which they may fail. If you continually put your own fears out there, your child might listen and never find something they love and succeed at. Or even worse, the athlete might lose the fun in it all.

Jack's mom never discouraged him from trying new things again. Her canned reply went from "I don't think that's a good idea" to "Ok, how will you accomplish that?"

Parental words and actions impact the athlete's environment more than parents realize. Choose the right encouraging words and send the message: Effort is key. Failure is inevitable, so learn from it and always focus on growth and learning. Remember, how *you* handle adversity or stress will also be noticed by your athletes. Make sure you send the right message to them to help develop character. I will repeat this throughout this book: the attributes we discuss, such as mindset, are learned through sport but are carried through life.

CHAPTER 3

Grit

It's the end of another recreational baseball season. After the game, the coach imparts some final words on his team as a mom waits in her car with a box of celebratory donuts. As her baseball player opens the car door and flops into the front seat, she hands him the box, "So how did it go?"

"We lost," he says, matter of fact, rummaging through the box.

The mom turns and looks out her windshield. She notices one of the team's best players walking off the field in tears. This player is followed by two other players who are having the same reaction.

"Kevin, what happened after the game?"

"Coach talked to us."

"What did he say?"

"He said, 'You're all a bunch of losers. I hope you have a better summer season.'"

"Did his talk upset you?"

"No, why?"

Now we could spend a considerable amount of time discussing the deplorable way the coach spoke to his players but that's not what's puzzling here. The lingering question is: why were some players affected by his words and others not? Specifically, why were Kevin's teammates crushed, while Kevin was seemingly unaffected? What drives an athlete to desire approval, even buckle under disapproval, and another seemingly not care about it?

I am happy to say, Kevin's love for baseball continues. He didn't let those damaging words by his coach rob him of his joy in continuing to play through middle school and into high school. Yet, all too often, this is not the case. Many athletes struggle with negative comments that linger in their minds and negatively affect their love of the game and their ability to perform.

When we witness parents or coaches outwardly berating an athlete after a bad game or practice, we understand the damage harsh words can inflict. However, what about the pressures we can't see? Parents often spend thousands on new equipment, elite teams, and personal coaches to develop their athletes—which can create a pressure cooker environment for some athletes. Those athletes who are not at the top of the playing field may consistently feel intense pressure to perform or move on either by their parents, coaches, or other teammates. The end result of these types of pressure is that kids leave sports and lose the social, physical, and academic benefits all too early.

There have been a multitude of articles and news reports on the high percentage of kids that leave organized sports by age 13. Most have stated their reasons as lack of fun because the pressures are too high either from parents, coaches, or other players. But I ask: Why just focus on the kids that leave organized sports to fix the problem? Why not look at the smaller percentage of youths that remain in sports? What keeps them in the sport when others give up? Is it that these athletes don't experience any negativity and have only experienced positivity and success? I doubt that. Look at the example above with the baseball player, Kevin. Do athletes like Kevin, who stick with the game, possess a trait the others do not?

We've learned from Dr. Nick the importance of mindset, learning how to look at failure in a positive light, but is that all that's needed to keep an athlete playing?

Dr. Nick

What propels someone to push himself or herself, to keep going amongst the obstacles, pressure, or negativity surrounding them? How do they push through to find the fun in their sport? Is it nature or nurture? What gives someone that singular focus to pursue excellence in performance? The simple answer: grit.

Canadian Brett Rheeder played hockey like many other Canadians but in his teens, Brett realized he didn't enjoy the team aspect of the sport (McNair, 2015). Brett abandoned hockey for mountain biking—his true passion. By age 16 he switched to slopestyle riding, which is downhill riding with jumps, half-pipes, and other obstacles. In 2009, he attended his first big competition in Colorado. Brett failed miserably. "I did horrible," he recalled. "I crashed in the first half hour of practice and was out the whole contest. That was a huge eye-opener for me, and I realized how tall of a ladder I had to climb-" (McNair, 2015).

But it wasn't that simple. Brett was coming from the farmlands of Canada where there were no mountains to train on. So, did he give up because the odds were against him? No. In fact, he figured out that he didn't need the mountains as much as he needed to be able to do the tricks. And practice the tricks he did. He and his friends even built a foam pit to train on (McNair, 2015).

But in 2013, after winning his first gold medal in the X-Games, Brett fractured his back in four places on his second run in the Crankworx Les 2 Alps (Rheeder, n.d.). He took time to recover and get back to training but returned to the sport he loved with the same passion and drive to succeed. In 2014, he ended up on the podium for the Red Bull Joyride. In 2015, Brett stunned with his impressive wins at Crankworx Rotorua Slopestyle and Crankworx Les 2 Alpes. "It was my second time back in Les Deux Alpes, since my back injury there in 2013, and also the first Crankworx I won where none of my competitors messed up or crashed. It was a straight-up win-" (Rheeder, n.d.).

This impressive Canadian mountain biker continues to pursue his passion today and is among the top slope style riders in the world.

Before the 1992 Olympic games in Barcelona, runner Derek Redmond, had already achieved world champion status (Redmond, 2012). But Derek had not had the perfect road to success. Having suffered many injuries, including one that kept him from competing in the 1988 Olympics, he worked tirelessly to qualify four years later. At the start of the 400-meter Olympic semifinal race, in which he was expected to take gold, he felt confident and physically ready. Yet, just after the race began, he heard a snap, felt searing pain and just like that, he could barely walk, let alone run. As he watched his competitors cross the finish line, he refused to give up. He didn't want it to go down in the record books that he, Derek Redmond, did not finish the race. So, he hobbled along the track toward the finish line in pain, knowing he had lost the race, yet refusing to quit.

From the stands, Derek's father emerged. The father ran to his son and told him he didn't have to finish. Derek recounts his father's words, "You're a champion, you've got nothing to prove-" (Redmond, 2012). But Derek wouldn't hear of it. He kept going, his dad by his side. When he finished the race, he received a standing ovation of 65,000 people (Redmond, 2012).

Brett Rheeder and Derek Redmond displayed grit in different ways: Brett's grit got him out of his bed and back on the bike. For Derek, he achieved the best he could with his injury, and he crossed that finish line like a true champion. Both athletes had the passion and perseverance to keep going in the face of adversity.

Are Brett and Derek unusual? No. Grit is demonstrated every day, from the mundane challenges to the extraordinary.

What Is Grit?

Have you ever been so physically exhausted that you wanted to drop right where you were, but you still had miles to go before you got to your destination? Have you had so much work piled up and a looming deadline that you wanted to put your head on your desk and cry? We have all had those moments when we didn't think we could see a task to the end and wanted to throw in the towel.

But sometimes we complete the tasks that initially seemed impossible, and we look back, amazed at having done it. If you've felt that way, you displayed grit—the ability to see the challenge, take it on, and complete the journey.

Grit doesn't just apply to athletics. Grit is necessary to see us over many hurdles in our lives. Helping a loved one through a severe illness, raising toddlers while holding down a full-time job, completing a 5k race after years of not running—whatever the challenge, grit was necessary to get the job done. Even the most gifted in our society will not achieve success in the absence of grit.

Brett Rheeder and Derek Redmond are just two examples out of millions we see every day—they can range from a tee ball player who finally makes contact with the ball at the last game of the season, to a pro golfer who wins a Major while his wife battles cancer. Grit is that inner voice which tells people to keep going despite any and all obstacles. That ability to dig deep into your gut and pull out what is almost lost.

However, for every athlete who perseveres, there are far more that give up; the flock of excuse makers who never achieve the excellence they desire or are capable of. This chapter is for them.

I cannot continue to explain my theory on grit without referencing the foremost authority on the subject, psychologist Angela Duckworth. Her years of study and research on this idea of grit is extraordinary and highly acclaimed.

In her book, *Grit: The Power of Passion and Perseverance,* Duckworth (2016) describes a test she developed while studying the attrition stats of new recruits from West Point, the United States Military Academy. Duckworth tested the West Point recruits to determine why some are able to stick it out and others leave. She used a grit test and a scale she had developed. In this 10-question test, she was able to determine the likelihood of a recruit to stay and complete his or her training at West Point.

Given West Point's rigorous acceptance requirements, the playing field is stacked with capable, talented, bright young men and women. These young adults are among the best of the best from high schools across the United States. What makes some of these individuals stay and finish, while others give up and leave? It clearly isn't from lack of talent, physical ability, or academic excellence. They all have it. So, what is it? What makes some quit, while others see it through to the end?

After her testing, Duckworth asserted that the recruits who make it to graduation do so because they possess grit. She sums grit up into two essential attributes: passion and perseverance (Duckworth, 2016).

I highly recommend you and your athlete each take the test on the following website: http://angeladuckworth.com/gritscale. This will give you a baseline grit score. Just note: Duckworth (2016) states that your grit scores can vary depending on when you take the test. Sometimes we possess more grit than others. Another key fact Duckworth makes very clear in her book is that "grit is mutable-" (Duckworth, 2016). How gritty you are can change (Duckworth, 2016). If your athlete has a low grit score, that can be changed. You can grow and develop a grittier character. So just remember where you or your child end up on the grit scale is just a place to start. Your score and your athlete's score can change for the better.

My definition of grit adds an additional component onto Duckworth's. Based on my work, with many athletes in all age and ability ranges, I find grit contains three key components: passion, perseverance, and a low need for positive reinforcement. Defining each individual element of grit facilitates understanding how they come together as one working unit and more importantly how to develop or enhance this attribute in a young athlete.

Passion, under my definition, is an intense experiential phenomenon directing the individual's spirit, life force, and energy towards a goal without hinderance of obstacles.

In practical terms, let's reference the example of Brett Rheeder (McNair, 2015). Most athletes, after a severe injury such as a broken back, might not return to the sport from fear alone. However, Brett had a deep internal drive to continue mountain biking and competing. It was that passion, that "governing force," that gave him intense focus to repair and to hone his physical skills, ultimately guiding him to multiple wins the following year.

Clearly, passion can be applied throughout our lives. We don't just have passion for sports. For example, the fact that you are reading this book speaks to a passion for being a good parent. Possessing that passion will push you to seek any means possible to help your child learn and grow properly, including reading this book.

Now, let's suppose the opposite were true, that you didn't care about parenting. Would you be driven to support your child or find ways to help them learn and develop? The answer is probably no. Some amount of passion is necessary for performance excellence, whether it's in sports or in another endeavor.

Passion can't be taught. As stated in the definition, it is visceral, an intrinsic motivation. Passion comes about naturally from within. You can't give someone passion or cultivate it the same way you can with other attributes. However, parents and coaches can play a role in identifying and sustaining an athlete's passion, as I will explain later in the chapter.

The second component in grit is perseverance. Perseverance is defined as, "continued effort to do or achieve something despite difficulties, failure or opposition-" (Merriam-Webster Dictionary, n.d.). If a child is learning to ride a bike, for example, and falls but gets back up and continues to try, they are showing perseverance. Individuals will fail at some point, but if failure is not a deal breaker for them, then they possess perseverance.

Typically, athletes with perseverance have a growth mindset. Remember, the growth mindset focuses on the process not the outcome; the battle not the victory (Dweck, 2016). An athlete with perseverance loves the game more than the win. They are driven by challenges, not results; the qualities of a growth mindset.

The most interesting and third component of my grit definition is the low need for positive reinforcement. A low need for positive reinforcement means that the person does not need to hear a positive statement from someone else to feel good about themselves or something they have done. If your athlete is constantly looking for praise or affirmation that their performance is good, then he or she has a high need for positive reinforcement and, under my definition, does not possess grit.

Why do I include a low need for positive reinforcement in my definition of grit where the leading expert on the subject matter does not? Because, in my clinical work, I have seen many clients who possess passion and perseverance, but their almost insatiable need for a parent's approval derails any grit they developed either through nature or nurture.

With a low need for positive reinforcement, if the individual wins or loses at something, they aren't seeking someone to tell them they are great, and they don't make up excuses for why they lost. Instead, there is a strong sense of self and a comfort with who they are and what they can do. How someone else views them holds little consequence to their performance.

Do not mistake this for arrogance. Arrogance is a feeling of superiority. A low need for positive reinforcement does not equate to an individual being haughty or aloof. Someone with low need for positive reinforcement simply owns their own truth and doesn't need, want, or seek approval.

For example, if your athlete is always looking to the sidelines for your smile or nod to fill their need for your approval, their focus in the game is jeopardized and thereby harming their performance. If, however, your athlete has a low need for positive reinforcement, their focus is on the task at hand, not what anyone else is thinking about his or her performance. If your athlete possesses a high need for positive reinforcement, it can be reduced. We will give you guidelines later in the chapter on how to reduce your athlete's need for positive reinforcement.

Note: Your child's temperament can impact positively or negatively this need for reinforcement. Typically, individuals who possess a more "easy-going" temperament have low sensitivity thresholds. By nature, they require less parental affirmation to feel good about their performance. Conversely, the "difficult" temperament holds higher sensitivity levels and requires larger amounts of positive reinforcement. Although we won't be able to change an athlete's innate temperament, we can alter their secondary reactions to stimuli—including their need for reinforcement—to produce better outcomes.

Just as Olympic runner Derek Redmond had passion and perseverance to make it across that finish line, he also possessed a low need for positive reinforcement. In an article, written by Redmond himself for the DailyMail.com, Redmond (2012) reports that he was unaware of anyone else, other than his father beside him, as he crossed the finish line. It wasn't until he finished and heard the crowd of 65,000 people giving him a standing ovation that he remembered they were there (Redmond, 2012). He didn't cross the line for anyone's approval, just his own.

Ask yourself: "Does my athlete have Dr. Nick's definition of grit with all three components?" "Have I fostered an environment that would encourage and support that attribute?" "Do I demonstrate passion and perseverance, without seeking constant approval in my work or in my role as a parent or coach?"

Think about your answers and be honest because they will matter as you read on. An athlete may not have grit now, but it can be fostered given the right environment.

Are All Three Components Necessary to Have Grit?

The aforementioned components are interdependent and crucial to fostering grit in any athlete. Without the presence of all three components, under my definition, grit is unattainable.

Perseverance is limited or non-existent in the absence of passion. Passion drives our ability to persevere. In order to keep going in the face of adversity, you have to be driven by a deep desire or passion. Would you be the next Ben & Jerry's if you hated ice cream, no matter how much you thought you could do it?

If the athlete possesses passion and perseverance, but has a high need for reinforcement, self-doubt will diminish their drive to conquer any challenge. If you're in the big game dribbling the ball down the court, but you're worried about what your parents are thinking, will you be able to take the ball to the net? Probably not with much success, if you keep looking up into the stands.

How to Nurture Grit

You can tell your athlete to stretch before the game, wear safety gear, or demonstrate good sportsmanship. You can encourage them to practice their physical moves for their sport: agility, balance, hand-eye coordination, etc. Yet, no matter how good those skills get or how high-quality the equipment, the athlete won't achieve excellence without grit.

Who knows more about grit than the Navy SEALs? The group's whole existence is based around the concept of grit (Barker, 2015). Trainees begin their training in BUD/S (Basic Underwater Demolition/SEAL) training: a seven-month endeavor that taxes an individual's mental and physical strength to their breaking points. This training is specifically designed to "weed" out those who won't make it through difficult challenges. Only the individuals who exhibit mental grit (passion, perseverance, and a low need for positive reinforcement) make it through training. The entire environment requires a high level of all three components, which are essential to becoming a Navy SEAL.

The SEALs who make it through BUD/S will spend at least 75% of their time training and the other 25% deployed. Developing their physical skills, along with a passion for what they do, is essential for a successful deployment (Barker, 2015). This should also be true for any athlete, as a high performance requires a strong mind and body.

Although SEALs are elite performers, they are not perfect. As I have stated already in this book, nothing is 100%100% of the time. In fact, after every mission, the team spends a large percentage of time debriefing on what they did wrong and how they can improve. They don't complete their missions looking for a pat on the back. SEALs love what they do, keep going under the almost insurmountable conditions, and come back wanting to be better for the next time. Isn't that what we should see in our athletes, both on and off the field? Isn't that the optimal goal?

So how do you get them there? How do parents instill grit into their child for athletics and beyond? Well, let's answer that using the three individual components, beginning with passion.

Passion is intrinsically driven, developed naturally. Yet, parents and coaches can impact the development of passion through the introduction of opportunities and modeling. Suggest your child tries different sports, and get them involved in activities they show interest in. Model passion yourself. Show them what it means to love something and pursue it with energy. Also, set time aside to watch or play sports together. This seemingly small thing provides much-needed encouragement for the athlete to try different sports or activities.

Keeping the aspect of sports fun and varied is key to longevity in any athletic endeavor. Our chapter on specialization will delve into this further. We will discuss the importance of playing many sports to cultivate interests and allow passions to develop on their own.

Perseverance, however, can be fostered when it is not present naturally. Some individuals are just born with it; others acquire it. Like any good life lesson, we can teach perseverance by showing. Help your athlete set goals for themselves in practice and competition. Perseverance is all about working toward those goals even in the presence of challenges. We will discuss goal setting in greater detail later on.

I had the pleasure of talking with a gentleman about youth sports and his own kids; his two boys played football in high school and currently play in college. He told me an interesting story about a time when his young sons were frustrated and ready to quit football, and how he turned their frustration into a teachable moment on perseverance.

During pee wee football (age ranges from 9 to 12) both his boys came to him with the questions: "Why can't we be the running backs? Why do we have to be in the defensive line?" This dad, whom I will refer to as Greg, happens to approach parenting in a more philosophical way by giving advice. The option of going to talk to the coach and making demands was never an option in his mind. Instead Greg directed his boys by saying, "Well boys, look who the coach is. His son is the running back."

His boys then said, "Then we are going to quit. Why can't you be the coach, Dad? You played college football!"

Greg responded, "No I'm not going to be the coach. You have to earn the position you want. If being a running back is what you really want, then earn it. You need to have the patience to stick it out, and learn the game from pee wee football. Figure out what you need to do to develop better skills and play better than everyone else because nobody's dad works for the high school."

"What do you mean?"

"Well, the high school football team is coached by a teacher, a gym coach, or someone that works for the high school, not someone's dad. High school is the great equalizer for many sports. You will excel based on your abilities, not who your parent is. Use this time to hone your skills and set your goals. When you get to high school, that's when you can demonstrate your abilities."

Greg then followed up with an example from his own youth sports experience: "Boys, Dad always loved baseball but when I was growing up, I wasn't the kid who played on travel or elite club teams. I strictly played recreational ball. When I got to high school, I knew my skill levels were good, so I tried out for the team. All the kids who played on travel and club teams asked what I was doing at try-outs. But you know what?"

"No, what?"

"I made the team. I knew I had the skills, and I made the team. And I played baseball all four years in high school. Hone your skills now and when you get to high school, you can go for that spot of running back or quarterback. Your hard work, patience, and perseverance will get you there. Not me being your coach and handing you a position."

The boys took the advice and stuck it out, and their abilities made them star running backs on their high school football team. They both went on to play football in college.

Now, my point of telling this story isn't to blast the dad who put his son in the coveted position, but to show how the dad of the two boys helped foster grit: setting goals and forcing them to achieve their goals on their own. Clearly, they had passion, but they needed to persevere to get to their end goal, to stick it out even when things weren't going their way. If you, like Greg, can teach that through words or actions, your athlete will eventually learn this skill for life.

It's crucial to explain how you excelled despite difficulties like Greg did. This will help your athlete understand that anything they desire takes work to achieve, and that in the end, you are better because of the work you put in. Let the athlete see that it's not only okay to fail, but that there is good that comes from it. Again, this takes time. It isn't one brief conversation at one time. This process will take time and repetition for it to become an embedded skill.

The third aspect of grit, a low need for positive reinforcement, can also be taught. First you must understand one principle: If you constantly praise every little thing, the athlete will look for it more and more to validate themselves. This praise becomes their drug to fuel their passion. This need eventually stifles grit's development, and the athlete will no longer be able to assess their performance accurately and be motivated to do better. Quite often this player is so busy looking for praise they are afraid to fail and pushing themselves is not an option.

Second, how you provide feedback can impact the level of need for positive reinforcement. Sports parents I come across today provide their athlete feedback typically in one of three categories: the brutally honest, the over embellisher of often unwarranted praise, and the parent who gives helpful, accurate, specific, and encouraging feedback. I am sure you know which one I will say is the healthiest and best for the athlete's continued growth and success. Clearly, it's the third one.

The parent who believes that brutal honesty with harsh tones and cutting words will inspire a child is misguided. All the athlete will get from cruel, overly harsh feedback is to develop a fear of failure. As we discussed in the chapter on mindset, fear can be their downfall or inability to reach their full potential (Dweck, 2006). Fear is the great destroyer of grit. It's essential the athlete understand failure is not the end. In fact, failure or poor performance should be presented as an important part of the learning process. A coach or a parent should never cast a poor performance as anything but a motivator to improve.

I recently saw a documentary about the infamous skater Tonya Harding.

For those of you unfamiliar with her story: In 1994 during the United States Figure Skating Championships, Harding's main rival was a skater named Nancy Kerrigan (Brodesser-Akner, 2018). After one of Nancy's practice sessions, a man clubbed her in the back of the knee. The man was Tonya's former bodyguard and a friend of her ex-husband. The details of the attack and her close connections to the perpetrator loomed as Tonya competed in the US Championship and in the Olympic Games the following month. She became the one to hate by almost everyone.

But this documentary focused on how the intense pressure while growing up led Tonya to this destination. How her feelings of being unloved and unsupported were a direct result of her mother's love being tied to Harding's performances. It's been alleged that her mother beat her when she didn't perform to expected standards, and so she developed a fear of failure (Brodesser-Aker, 2018).

When Tonya performed poorly, she would immediately blame it on outside factors: her skates weren't working right, the ice was bad, or whatever she could point to as a distraction. And when all the cards were stacked against her in the Olympic Games, amidst the allegations of her involvement of the Kerrigan attack, she crumbled under the pressure (Brodesser-Aker, 2018). At the beginning of her performance she made a tearful plea to the judges claiming she broke a lace ("The Oregonian, 1994). The judges allowed her to restart her performance as the last skater that day, but she landed only three out of the six planned jumps. Her poor performance landed her in 8th place that year ("The Oregonian", 1994). And, in the end, Tonya never returned to skating.

Yes, this is an extreme case, but it is in extreme cases we see truths that can act as inspiration or cautionary tales for the masses. The take-away is clear: The choices we make in parenting directly affect the present and future lives of our children. Being overly critical and tying parental affection to an athlete's performance can reduce any athlete's performance, in sports and life.

But what about the positive parents who are all sunshine and roses? Those that embellish praise on their child, warranted or not, such as: "You are fabulous!" "You're the best one on the team!" "You would have won today, but that other kid distracted you." "It wasn't your fault, the other player got lucky, and the weather was working against you." "Your coach didn't give you the right advice."

These parents may be on the opposite side of the spectrum from the brutally honest parent, yet the end results are often the same. These parents find it all too difficult to allow their children to feel they've failed at anything. They embellish their successes and downplay or dismiss their failures to prevent their children from feeling badly about themselves. They never want their athlete to experience any negative emotions, perhaps because they themselves know how difficult those feelings are, or because they feel it's their job as a parent to protect. No matter the motive, intervening to prevent disappointment for an athlete robs them of learning critical coping skills.

Oftentimes, these overly positive parents come into my office with a laundry list of reasons why their child didn't perform his or her best during a competition. These parents are well meaning. However, their protective nature can kill future growth for their athletes because they're not allowing the athlete to accurately assess their weaknesses and develop the motivation to fix them. The protected athletes never develop perseverance and constantly seek approval or make excuses. They too end up developing a fear of failure and never push themselves beyond the safe zone of their abilities.

The parents who can give positive and negative feedback with specific, helpful critiques, using growth-minded words, will have a greater chance of developing an athlete with grit. Their athletes won't fear failure or avoid pushing themselves because they'll see failure as part of the learning and development process to becoming a higher performer. In fact, this athlete will feed off a bad performance, working harder and smarter to achieve better results the next time with little to no concern for reinforcement.

Your six-year-old is playing baseball. Each Saturday you pack the cooler and folding chairs in the car. One Saturday, you ask the grandparents to join—a picture perfect memory, or so you anticipate. A player hits the ball and it rolls to your kid, who is playing in the sand at first base. Your first baseman bends over and picks up the ball. The batter runs to the base and right into your kid who's holding the ball up for you to see he had it. You shake your head as your first baseman and batter talk as if they were the best of friends.

Instantly your own father stands up and yells, "Hey, he's out!"

Immediately you jump up, "Dad, be quiet. There are no outs."

"No outs, then what kind of game are we playing?"

The mother, sitting next to you, leans over and gently tells the grandparent, "Everyone bats, and no one ever gets out."

Gramps, not backing down, replies, "Then how do you know who wins?"

The woman gasps, and snaps, "There are no winners or losers, it's always a tie!"

"What?" your father yells loud enough to stop the game.

Besides it being the last time you invite Grandpa to the game, you secretly wonder if he might be right. Are all these attempts to make everyone a winner harmful to a child's inner drive?

The answer to the above story is a definitive yes. Too much unwarranted positivity is disingenuous and easily readable by the youngest of children. Keep your feedback accurate and specific. Foster a sense of fun, pride, and accomplishment without embellishment. Make any reinforcement constructive and pointed. Tell them, "I like the way you took the club back" or "I liked the way you passed the ball to your teammate." Specific critiques assist the athlete and do not foster any need for the proverbial pat on the back. The athlete will instead rely on himself or herself to achieve their goal. Just as we saw in the baseball story at the beginning of this chapter, in which Kevin's coach used cruel and overly harsh words. Kevin didn't need a coach to use positive words to keep his love of the game going. In fact, those words had little to no impact on Kevin's passion for the game.

Failure's Impact on Grit

External factors such as success or failure can directly affect grit—specifically, the passion aspect of it. The link between passion and performance can be powerfully interdependent. Success can increase passion levels, where failure can negatively impact passion levels. Sometimes the hardest part of grit is maintaining passion in the wake of failure.

Again, we go back to mindset as an essential attribute supporting many other important attributes like grit. The growth-minded individual will have an easier time maintaining their passion, even when there are setbacks. Growth-minded individuals will see failure as an opportunity to grow. Mistakes, playing poorly, and losing are just parts of learning for the growth-minded individual, making the correlation between passion and performance low to non-existent. Whereas, the fixed-minded individual's performance will significantly impact their passion.

As previously discussed, the Navy SEALs go over their mistakes after a mission in an effort to improve (Barker, 2015), indicating that they too are growth minded, just as Rheeder and Redmond are. Even in the face of defeat, their high passion levels did not take a significant hit. It's this very attitude that parents need to instill in their athletes and no time like the present. No athlete is too young or too skilled to learn this essential thought process.

As in the earlier story about the Kevin, where his baseball coach critiqued the team with harsh and cruel words, we have to ask: Why were Kevin's teammates crushed and Kevin seemingly unaffected? The simple answer is grit. Kevin's parents never overreacted to his smallest of accomplishments or gave him false accolades. He never developed the need to continuously seek out compliments, especially when he knew he didn't deserve them. They did, however, give specific, accurate feedback, both positive and negative, directing and encouraging him to work at his weaknesses to improve his performance.

When Kevin experienced failure, his parents would consistently say, "Well, what did you learn and what will you do to make it better next time?" They put the ownership in his hands to grow and learn. It's also important to note that their tone and the way they addressed Kevin's failures or successes were never over the top to the negative or positive. There was never a link between their love and his performance at any time.

Of course, Kevin is also quite growth minded, so that particular loss didn't destroy or damage his passion for baseball. Because of his growth mindedness, along with his parent's handling of his previous failures and successes, Kevin didn't crumble that day or any day in the future. He is still playing baseball in high school, several years after this incident and his passion level for the game remains intact.

For the athlete who possesses grit, failure acts as a motivator. They are charged with energy through what they have learned from failure. Typically, they will hit it harder at practice, replay the events that brought them down, and critique their opponent's performance to grow and learn. The athlete with grit learns and gets better from failure, just as we saw with Kevin.

Conversely, the athlete who doesn't have grit typically has a fixed mindset and crumbles from failure, just like Tonya Harding did. They can't rebound, lose the passion they once had, and oftentimes play the blame game. You ask what went wrong, and they list a million reasons why: the weather, the conditions weren't right, the other player had an advantage, they didn't feel well, and on and on.

What do you do about the athlete who crumbles when he or she fails? You need to create an environment that focuses on perseverance and constructive reinforcement. Help them set new goals, with specific plans to achieve them and a constant stream of constructive feedback, where your critiques are focused on the specifics of their performance.

Grit is critical for engaging the athletic powerhouse that is one's mind. Excellence in performance only thrives in the existence of grit, just as grit survives because of a growth mindset. Again, every attribute or resource I introduce is co-dependent on another; one strength alone will not create a strong mental game for any athlete.

CHAPTER 4

Goal Setting

There isn't a sport parent out there that hasn't had one or more of "those days." There's homework to finish, a dog to walk, dinner to prepare (the roast is still frozen), and your athlete is frantically trying to find a lost mouth guard or glove. By the time you leave, you are ten minutes late to the practice field, one meltdown behind you, unfinished homework on the table, and no dinner in sight. You slam the car door, and you mutter in frustration as your athlete whines, "Do I have to go to practice?"

"Yes, you have to go!" Exasperated, you retell a story you recently saw on television, with marked intensity, as if you were narrating a 48 Hours episode. "This winter, a high school basketball team from Iowa won a championship game in the final seconds of the last quarter. The two boys that made the winning play were interviewed after the game. You know what they said?"

You look and wait for your now pouting child to shake their head.

"That luck had nothing to do it. They said they earned the win because of long hours of practice. And they didn't just go to practice, they set goals and did specific drills to accomplish them. That's how they improved and were able to win." Point made.

As adults and parents, no one has to convince us of the power of practice. We get it because we've lived it, and we preach it at every turn. But as our child matures and gets deeper into their sport, the conflict morphs from the question "Do I have to practice?" into a never-ending debate on 'how' to practice. We start conveying the idea of working smarter while emphasizing quality.

In an effort to support our points, we purchase a multitude of training aids, with anticipation that our athlete will make their way to the back yard to hone their skills. Daily, we ask them if they actually used that pitch back, goalie net, or chipping net we mow around each week. No judgment here—the things Golf Galaxy has that my home doesn't are a neon sign and parking lot.

I understand that legends like Michael Jordan, Tiger Woods, and Derek Jeter didn't make it because of their apparatus or the latest equipment. So, I wonder: *What makes a practice truly productive?*

Dr. Nick

Practice makes perfect—isn't that what we've been taught, and what we preach? This notion of the more time you practice, the greater your chance for success. But what about the adage: Work smarter not harder? The second is the antithesis of the first and yet, I hear parents and coaches mutter both to their players consistently. What if both adages contain considerable merit? An athlete's view on practice should include both time and purpose to produce excellence in performance.

It's not uncommon for parents to complain to me that their child doesn't practice effectively, but merely goes out and mindlessly does whatever drills they feel like for too short an amount of time. My advice is this: Time is important, the athlete's focus and intention during that time is more important, and goal setting is *most* important.

Many athletes, like Tiger Woods, Kobe Bryant, Michael Jordan, and Jerry Rice, just to name a few, have well-documented, intense practice routines. Their practices contained, first and foremost, specific goals coupled with incredible, never-give-up work ethic. They combined time and purpose into their practice to achieve excellence. Not unlike our example of the Navy SEALs who spend 75% of their time practicing for 25% time deployed (Barker, 2015).

If you drive to work and have no plan for the day, are you going to be as productive as you would be if you had goals established to accomplish certain tasks? Absolutely not. The most productive people I know are the ones who have set goals throughout their days as a matter of course. Goal setting comes as natural to them as breathing does. Individuals who set goals for themselves intrinsically understand that productivity is the precursor to success.

Again, let me reiterate: time is important, the athlete's focus and intention during that time is more important, and goal setting is *most* important. Therefore, this chapter will begin by explaining the highly effective and very specific process of setting goals before any practice. Then, I will explain how we take an athlete's overall goal and create a plan to achieve it. Once you understand the goal setting process, I will give you specific techniques to use in practice for your athlete to achieve both physical and mental goals.

Goal Setting

Effective or productive practice does not exist in the absence of goal setting. Goal setting is the key ingredient to a productive practice. In order to appropriately goal set, it's not enough to say, "I want to be the best at foul shots or to make more foul shots this year." Those statements represent wishes. True goals require commitment and an organized, well-designed plan. Athletes, no matter their age, must set goals with an organized, well-thought-out plan to achieve them.

For example, let's say you want that new hot car that just came out. If you say, "I want to get that car next year." Is that a goal? No, at that point, it's just a wish. Seeing this as a goal is where many people make a mistake. It's not a goal until you have made a plan and are committed to getting there. Until you have said, "I want to get this car next year, so I will save x amount over the next twelve months," and then specifically design how you will save and commit to it, this is nothing more than a wish. So, how do we turn a wish into an achievable goal?

It is a commonly acceptable practice to look at goal setting with three essential components or levels: Outcome, performance, and process.

The first level of goal setting is the outcome. This is the overall objective the athlete wants to achieve. For example, a college basketball player may want to increase the number of three-point shots made in a game and that will become his outcome goal—the end-all objective the athlete is working toward.

The performance goal is the way to measure the goal. So, if the outcome goal is to increase the amount of three-pointers made in a game, then the performance goal may be increasing the percentage of shots made in practice from 35% to 45%.

The process goal is the specific drill or exercise the athlete does to achieve his or her performance goal. In our example, to achieve the outcome goal of making more three-point shots, the athlete set a performance goal of making 45% of three-point shots taken. The process goal could be to shoot three-point shots from multiple positions on the court for a greater amount of time each practice session.

When Earl Woods would practice with Tiger, they set goals for Tiger to increase his focus. To make sure Tiger could be hyper focused during competitive rounds, Earl would create distractions during practice sessions (Fields, 2006). The outcome goal was for Tiger to be hyper focused. The performance goal was based on how many times he remained focused during distractions. The process goal was for Tiger to complete various practice rounds with varied distractions that would occur at random times.

Clearly the goal setting and practice paid off, because Tiger became known for his ability to be hyper focused in competition. He seemed to block out distractions with ease.

Below is a chart depicting how those three goals should flow and affect each other.

GOAL SETTING

Once a player sets the outcome goal, they determine the performance goal—how the goal will be measured. The process goal is then a drill specifically designed to enhance the player's skills necessary to achieve the performance goals. As the performance goals are met, the outcome goals are achieved.

Let's revisit the car example. You had a wish for a new car. Now you set a goal of getting a new car in twelve months which became your outcome goal–the overall objective. Next you planned to save a certain amount in the next twelve months, which became your performance goal. To achieve that monetary measurement of your performance goal, you planned to cut expenses by a specific percent each month by giving up dinners out at expensive restaurants—and that became your process goal. You committed to that process goal, you achieved your performance goal of saving the money, and you achieved your outcome goal of buying your dream car.

Once you can get your athlete to understand and employ this process of goal setting, practices will be more productive, and they will grow as an athlete physically and mentally. The skill of goal setting will naturally transcend into other areas of the athlete's life because with repetition it will be imbedded into how they approach challenges.

Set Appropriate Goals

There is no difference between how a youth player practices and how a professional athlete practices; all levels of players practice basic skills. No one ever masters basic skills. Remember: nothing is 100%, 100% of the time. Therefore, goal setting works for all levels of athletes and is imperative to enhancing a player's skill set.

But if all players, no matter their age or ability, practice basic skills, are their goals the same in definition and approach? No, they aren't. Let's look at it this way: You have a ten-year old and a collegiate player both setting an outcome goal to increase their goal percentage; does it mean they should have the same performance and process goals? Absolutely not. Goals are player specific. Age and skillset are factors that must be considered when establishing goals at each level: outcome, performance, and process.

For example, a seven-year-old's golf practice should not include lifting weights—that would be physically inappropriate—or hitting 9 out of 10 shots perfectly from a basket of 90 practice balls daily—that would be an impossible task. Those goals may work for an older athlete with a more developed skill set.

The Challenge-Skills Balance chart below shows how an appropriate balance between challenges and skills directly impacts the player's mental game to the negative or positive. That means that although the athlete is challenged, if that challenge isn't appropriate for their skills, the effects on their mental game can be detrimental.

Challenge-Skills Balance

Csikszentmihalyi, 1977

In the upper right quadrant, the athlete's challenge is high, and their skills are high. Athletes who are highly challenged in a way that's appropriate for their skill level will respond with more focus and will achieve what is called a "flow" state. "Flow" state is not a relaxed emotional state but one where the athlete is self-efficacious (discussed in detail later on), focused, and performing at their best–physically and mentally.

In the upper left quadrant, the player's anxiety is high because the challenge is inappropriately high for their skill set. This is when the player wants to rise to the challenge, but the challenge is unrealistic for their current level and produces anxiety. Anxiety can cripple a player from developing and growing because their focus shifts from the task to fear of not reaching their goal.

In the bottom right quadrant, where the skills are high but the challenge is low, the player can end up feeling bored. Boredom, like anxiety, is insidious to growth and development. The bored player can become stagnant and will not feel inspired to increase their skill level, in turn never reaching their full potential or any goal they may have set.

Players who are in the lower left quadrant have challenges that are low but so are their skills. With the low skill set in hand, a player needs something to spark desire to better themselves. Specifically, if the lower challenge doesn't give enough to motivate or incite the low skill set to improve, apathy will set in. The player will stagnate, and these players often leave the sport.

So, what is this telling us? In any practice, the challenges must be appropriate for a player's skill level and provide enough motivation for the player to push themselves and grow their skills as a player. However, as the chart depicts, if this balance is off significantly, then the emotional game of a player can be negatively impacted. Once the player is in a negative emotional state, such as apathy, boredom, or anxiety, their ability to achieve performance excellence is compromised–at times significantly. So, challenge the players in practice and competition but do so appropriately to their capabilities.

The first step in establishing appropriate practice goals with your athlete is having an open and relaxed discussion. Goals should never be made by you, the parent or coach, and then handed to the athlete. Pushing goals onto the player may work on some goals in the short term but will never work in the long run. Research has shown that goals are more likely to be achieved in the existence of ownership. The athlete must "own" the goal setting practice while parents and coaches simply guide them.

You're probably wondering: How does a parent get their athlete to take ownership of their goal setting? It's important to address goal setting in a pointed, age-appropriate conversation, when the moment allows for it. Pick a time when you have your athlete's complete attention, so that a calm, insightful discussion can occur without pressure. Remember you want the goals to come from the athlete. A conversation might sound like this:

PARENT: Wouldn't you agree that most professional athletes set goals?

CHILD: I guess.

(The question is set up as a way to introduce the thought. No matter how the athlete answers, you are ready with your follow up)

PARENT: Yes, they do set goals.

(You knew the answer to the question and now the thought process is introduced to your athlete).

PARENT: Why do you think they set goals?

CHILD: I don't know. Maybe to do better?

PARENT: Professional athletes establish goals to keep improving and challenging themselves to do better and be better. Don't you think all athletes, no matter what age or level, should do that?

CHILD: Yes

PARENT: Where would you like to improve? What are some goals you think you should have?

This will get the discussion going and hopefully establish some outcome goals. An outcome goal could be making more shots, improving their time, or making the high school team for example. Once the outcome goal is established, you can then follow up with questions regarding where your child feels they need to improve in order to achieve their overall goals—emphasizing that need for improvement is part of the process, not something to fear or be embarrassed about. This will help you guide your child to setting appropriate performance and process goals. Again, they have to own this process for it to work. Do not do it for them, simply guide them.

Set Obtainable and Measurable Goals

Beware: before you let your athlete set a goal and call it a day, you have to be sure the goals they set for themselves are obtainable and can be measured. This requires some thought. Keep the goal within their grasp but challenging at the same time.

Each of the three levels of goals—outcome, performance, and process—must be included in goal setting. They must also be attainable and measurable. Attainability means the goal can be reached given their physical capability and within a reasonable time frame. Measurability refers to clearly defined parameters where a baseline is known, and the goal can be gauged.

If the goal is not attainable within a reasonable amount of time or you can't measure it to conclude whether it's been reached or not, then the player risks feeling discouraged, potentially losing motivation and passion. No one wants that result. Again, we need to use the right words to direct the athlete in the right direction.

Here is an example:

PARENT: *What kind of goal do you think you should set?*

CHILD: *I want to be a professional basketball player.*

PARENT: *Ok, that's great. But you have a lot of years before that can happen. Do you think Michael Jordan just had becoming a pro-ball player as his only goal?*

CHILD: *I don't know.*

PARENT: *Well, he didn't. That may have been his ultimate future goal, but as he was developing as a player, he had smaller, more specific goals set for himself along the way. What do you think you need to work on right now to keep growing as a player?*

CHILD: *I'm really bad at foul shots.*

PARENT: *Ok, so do you think that you should make that a goal for the next three practices—improve the number of shots you make at the foul line?*

CHILD: *Yes*

PARENT: *Then how should we measure it, to be sure you are reaching that goal?*

CHILD: *Well, Jack on my team is good at them and Coach said he makes four out of every five foul shots he takes.*

PARENT: *So, do you think that should be your goal? Let's say over the next four practices?*

CHILD: *Sure*

PARENT: *Good. What kind of specific practices should you focus on to make that happen?*

CHILD: *I never try those shots in practice because I know I'm bad. So, maybe I need to shoot from the foul line for twenty shots a day for the next week. And make sure I use the backboard as my target, that's what coach always says.*

PARENT: *Good. It sounds like a solid goal. By the end of next week let's see if you have reached your goal of four out of five foul shots.*

In that sample conversation, the parent has helped the child set their out-come, performance, and process goals for the next week. The risk of the child not achieving it is low. One, the athlete owns it and two, the goal is both attainable and measurable. My next advice for this parent would be to make sure they follow up and immediately have the child set another goal. The more frequently goals are set by the athlete, the more embedded the process will become in his or her life. The ultimate result for goal setting should be for the process to become as natural as breathing.

Critical Follow-up, Distractions and Pitfalls

Now the above scenario is ideal, but it's important to understand that success isn't guaranteed even if the goals set are appropriate, attainable, and measurable. First, life happens. Even with the best-laid plans, scenarios arise and a well-developed plan can fall apart. Second, athletes can get frustrated or overwhelmed with other responsibilities or they can simply lose interest. How do we instill this critical process of goal setting amongst all the other distractions and pressures in life? The easy answer is to not give up, show the grit we talked about earlier. You accomplish this by always following up with a conversation to evaluate the goal—whether it's achieved or not. Do not just drop the subject because the goal wasn't reached and hope for a better result next time.

With each goal your athlete establishes, set a specific timeline for achieving that goal. At the end of that timeline, no matter how the plan was executed, there must be a review of the specific achievement or failure to reach the goal. If you set a goal and never talk about why it worked or why it didn't, you have severely injured the goal setting process for your athlete and made future goals harder to achieve. It doesn't matter if they exceeded their goal, made the goal, or completely failed to achieve their goal; the review process is as critical as setting the goal.

During this review process, the parent should be alert to the answers they get from the child. First, athletes who don't reach their goals, fail for many reasons: goals were unattainable for their age and skill level, they have too many pressures from other areas of life, they fear failure, or they are bored. Whatever the reason, parents and coaches need to help the athlete determine why they dropped the pursuit or failed to reach the goals they themselves established.

Parents and coaches often say to me, "Well, my child had goals but then lost interest in them." Or "They never followed through with the practice plan toward reaching those goals." Or "They lost interest and had a million excuses and didn't follow through." Generally, what I take from comments such as those is that the goals were abandoned without addressing the real reasons why, possibly because the parent or coach didn't hear what the athlete was saying.

Quite often when parents or coaches get frustrated with the athlete discussing why he or she hasn't achieved their goal, they fail to hear the athlete. They listen to what the athlete says verbally, but they miss the often-subtle clues the athlete is giving them. Specifically, when dealing with children from a young age to teens, they may not spell out the issue in a clear concise manner. They don't come to us and state: "I feel overwhelmed. I feel too much pressure. I am afraid of failing." However, what does happen is they fail to verbalize their feelings and oftentimes become emotional. Stop the conversation at that point. If you or your athlete is getting frustrated, stop and revisit the conversation when you both can discuss it calmly.

Be sure to watch their body language as well. You know your child best and you can pick up clues from how their voice changes or how they hold their posture, and so on. Once you hear what they are saying verbally and non-verbally, put yourself in their shoes. I talk about this all the time, a parent or coach must be empathetic and see the child's world through their eyes to find out what is really going on. This is not an easy task, but it is crucial.

For example, let's suppose the athlete in the last parent/child conversation example didn't reach his goal of achieving four out of five foul shots he made in basketball.

PARENT: *Well, it's been a week. Did you reach your goal of 4 out of 5 foul shots?*

CHILD: *No.*

PARENT: *Why do you think that is?*

CHILD: *I had too much homework this week and then Mom signed me up for more piano lessons and then I had CCD class. I didn't have time to shoot every day!*

At this point, the child might be showing frustration through his or her tone or physical movements. Just continue to listen. Take a deep breath and try to calm the situation by showing them you have empathy for them. You might say:

PARENT: *Ok, I get it. I know what it's like to have a packed schedule. So, let's think about some ways you can manage your time better so that you can reach your goal?*

If you find yourself having a similar conversation to this one, this is your opportunity to help your athlete learn to manage his or her time and prioritize. Let the athlete take the lead in the decisions about how they might manage their time more effectively. Be their guide. Keep the outcome goal in the forefront, so they can make the changes to achieve their goal and achieve the excellence they want.

The more success they have, the greater the motivation to keep achieving. Success is its own motivator.

For more potential dialogue to use, go back to the chapter on mindset and use the growth-minded vocabulary when you talk with your child about goal setting, the effectiveness of it, and the results. Be open, honest, and supportive. Remember, what a parent says is just as important as how they say it.

Grit's Impact of Goals

I often caution parents against assuming the cause of their athlete not meeting a goal was due to boredom or that the athlete wasn't motivated enough or even that the goal was set too low. Many times, parents and coaches will either raise the goal to attempt to instill a greater motivational level or provide what I call the "dangling carrot"—a reward or bribe—an outside motivator for the athlete to achieve a goal. This almost never works, leaving many goals unfulfilled and athletes achieving far less than excellence.

Countless times, I've witnessed a parent offer grandiose gestures if a specific goal is achieved: "I'll get you the new set of irons you want if you win your first AJGA event." Or "If you shut out every goal in the next game, I will buy you the new iPhone you wanted." Those rewards or bribes rarely, if ever, work. They rob the athlete of achieving their own sense of accomplishment by reaching a goal they set for themselves. The success of reaching a set goal should be the reward.

The more effective, proven method of goal achievement is what is called the Nike method; "Just Do It." Sound simplistic? It should, because it is and to understand what I am getting at, let's revisit the topic of grit and the importance of that attribute for success in athletics and beyond.

Grit is defined as containing three key components: passion, perseverance, and a low need for positive reinforcement. Note, all three components must be present for an individual to have grit. If an athlete has grit, the goal setting process won't be enhanced by an outside motivator. The athlete will be motivated by his or her own passion, perseverance, and low need for positive reinforcement. The athlete with grit will "Just Do It."

Effective goal setting requires setting appropriate, attainable, and measurable goals, followed by the critical evaluation process and the immediate setting of new goals. It is an iterative process, meaning the athlete is continuously in a state of adjusting, increasing, and modifying their goals and practices to achieve them. Goal setting requires grit and a growth mindset for the athlete to hold on to their overall objective. The more success the player gets, the more self-efficacy is developed and the more the practice of goal setting is embedded.

CHAPTER 5

Practice

Like most sports parents, I've attended too many practices to count and most of them I can't recall with much clarity, except for one. It happened in arctic-like temperatures in mid-April. Not surprisingly, on this practice round, we had the golf course all to ourselves as the precipitation switched from rain to snow, back to rain. By the second hole, I wanted to hightail it back to the car, blast the heat, and defrost my extremities. My golfer remained focused. He took advantage of the vacancy to belabor every shot for all 18 holes. My teeth chattered as I sipped my once-hot coffee, but I didn't race back to the car because I appreciated the focus my child brought to the table that day.

Forty-eight plus hours later, he one putted for birdie on a play-off hole and won. At home, I gently pointed out the correlation between the practice round productivity and his success. In his usual, often subtle manner, he gave me a smile and a nod. And I wondered: *How could his practices take on this level of focus all the time?*

Dr. Nick

So many times, I hear parents ask how they can get their athlete to practice more effectively and on a consistent basis. As with everything else, nothing is 100%, a 100% of the time. Therefore, not all practices are created equally, and consistency in practice is often difficult to achieve. Let's take a step back and remember what I stated in the previous chapter referent to skill development: Time is important, focus and intention is more important, and goal setting is most important. But how does that transfer into consistent and effective practices?

Time, focus, intention, and goal setting are most successful when deep, deliberate practice is utilized. Deep, deliberate practice is a key method for an athlete to take a process goal and break it down to the most basic component the athlete needs to improve to gain the desired performance and outcome goal.

To understand what I mean, let's take an example of a basketball player who established an outcome goal of increasing their three-point shots with a performance goal of making 90% of the shots. Let's say the athlete created a process goal of practicing these shots for longer periods and from different angles. Now, if that same athlete employs a deep, deliberate practice method, they will take the process goal to the next level. They will drill down and determine which basic skill, associated with shooting, they need to improve in order to reach their performance and outcome goals.

To do this, the athlete will need to determine which basic skill needs improving to make more of the shots, such as: form, always having a strong base, making sure they follow-through, and so on. For this example, we will say the athlete determined his form is weak. So, deep, deliberate practice will be practicing three-pointers with the athlete focused on keeping the proper shooting form.

So, at this point, will the athlete just focus on form and randomly shoot three-point shots from various positions? Not with deep, deliberate practice. Achieving the goal is the prime objective; however, it's equally important that the skill needed to accomplish a goal is not fleeting but implanted in the athlete. In deep, deliberate practice there is a process called embedding. Embedding has the athlete practice the specific skill using a series of training blocks to ensure the skill isn't temporary.

Here's how it works: You practice one skill, such as form, under a parameter (one shooting position on court) for a specific amount of time. Then you practice the same skill under another parameter (a different position on the court) for another block of time and so on. Then, to enhance the learning of that skill, the skill is then performed under varied parameters (all of the positions) for another block of time. The skill (form) is the constant and the parameters (court positions) are variable. This method will embed the skill into the mind of the athlete much more effectively than just practicing the one skill over and over under a constant parameter.

To clarify further, let's look at another example. A young golfer sets an outcome goal to reduce his number of putts during competition. The performance goal is to sink x number of putts on the practice green while putting from different distances. Each distance is for a specified period of time. Now to make that practice deep and deliberate, the golfer might putt with a specific focus on the putting stroke. To embed the specific stroke, the player's focus on the stroke will remain constant and the distance from the hole will vary for a specific block of time (parameter), with the last block of time varying the distances.

Introduction of Pressure

Once a skill is embedded for the athlete, deep, deliberate practice can and should take the method one step further by altering the environment. It's not enough to say the skill is mastered and the athlete should be fine in competitive situations. There is a mental game aspect that competition brings that does not exist in most practices: pressure. The environment for any practice should, at some point, exhibit the element of pressure.

So, how is that done? Let's look at our golfer scenario. Once the skill of making the proper stroke and sinking more putts is achieved, the next step would be to introduce pressure. Pressure in practice must be similar to the pressure of competition. In this example, the practice would then have the athlete sink x number of putts on each of the three practice holes. *But*, if there is a missed putt, the player goes back to the beginning and pressure has been introduced. Again, I can't impress upon this enough but pressure, like that in competition, is key to performance preparation.

To recap, the athlete must set their goals—defining the outcome, performance, and process goals. And in order to achieve a higher level of skills, goals and practice drills must be appropriate for the athlete, as we previously discussed. Next, the most effective way for the athlete to achieve a goal is through deep, dedicated practice where pressure is ultimately introduced. This process is iterative and infinite but crucial to learn for success in sports and life, no matter what path your athlete chooses.

Mental Game Practice

Often parents and athlete's alike ask: "Is the mental game all that important if an athlete has good physical skills?" The answer is a definitive yes. The athlete can be the most physically capable athlete but if their mind is processing anxiety, looking for constant reassurance, or just unfocused, then they won't be able to perform with excellence.

Let's first define what I mean by the player's mental game. The mental game for an athlete is what happens inside the player's mind during practice or competition. What are they telling themselves? How are they reacting to what is being said and done by coaches, other players, and parents? Where is their focus?

An athlete's mental game is reflective of their social intelligence or awareness. Social intelligence or awareness relates to the ability to assess one's environment. For the athlete, that is the playing field, which can include other players, where the puck or ball is, where they should be on the field, and so on. If a player doesn't understand the playing field or can't anticipate what could occur during play or how they should react to it, they will be at a significant disadvantage. No matter what their physical skill set is, if they have low to no levels of awareness or social intelligence, the player will not perform to their full potential. High levels of social intelligence for your athlete should be the goal, but be careful, high levels require something you can't give your athlete: passion.

High passion levels drive a high social intelligence. The more passion a player has for a sport, the greater their intention during performance: If an athlete's passion is high, their intention will be high—it's a one-to-one correlation. Intention drives attention or focus. Therefore, a high level of passion will produce a more focused player and thus, a higher level of social intelligence.

Is that to say that the athlete who plays soccer for fun, socialization, or physicality but holds a low level or no passion for it will *never* be able to increase their focus or awareness? Absolutely not. Social intelligence can be increased despite the level of passion or lack of it. However, those with high passion levels will naturally possess higher social intelligence and are the better, more focused, higher achieving players.

An athlete can increase their social intelligence or awareness, based on how they practice. Practicing self-awareness should happen on and off the field in order to properly embed this skill.

To begin any practice for awareness, have the athlete focus on one particular intention. For example, you could ask them to pay attention for a shooter coming across the middle or concentrate on the ball once it strikes the bat or block out distractions as they swing. Pick one thing they need to concentrate on and set specific awareness goals with each practice or game. The outcome goal should be to have their attention rise to a level between eight and 10, on a one-to-10 scale.

In addition to practicing awareness during play, athletes can enhance their awareness at other times throughout the day. Performing awareness exercises are easy and not very time intensive. You can have your athlete look at something in the room they are sitting in, for example. Once they have something specific in mind, ask them to look at it again but with intention, meaning looking at the object specifically focusing on each detail. Then ask them to explain what they saw differently. Doing this simple exercise throughout the day will naturally train their subconscious mind to start looking at things with more intention or focus.

Training the brain to see the small details will help transfer over to sports. The player who is hyper aware of their surroundings will notice the small details like what an opponent's body placement is saying about their next move or how an opponent is showing frustration and how that can be used to their benefit.

Let's try something different. Take a minute and think about your favorite room in your house. Sweep that room in your mind. Hold that thought. Now sweep the room again but with intention, or deeper focus. Did you find something different? Did you look at it with greater awareness around the small details like paint color, wall art, or the windowsills that need cleaning? I bet you did. Try this exercise with your player as well to practice and increase their awareness.

Have you ever read a paragraph and forgotten what you read? I venture to guess you have, since it happens to everyone. What would happen if you read a paragraph but, before you started, you said to yourself, "I will read this and identify the most important sentence in this paragraph?" Would you remember what you read then? Yes, you would. When you read with intention you pay attention. Our attention is driven by our intentions. If you approach anything with intention, your attention or awareness will be higher.

One of my clients is a collegiate soccer player. Unfortunately, she was in jeopardy of losing her spot on the team if her kicks didn't produce an additional five to eight yards consistently. The athletic ability to kick farther was there. Her coach knew she had the capability and so did I.

When I met with her, I asked, "When you kick, what is your thought process or intention?"

"I'm usually thinking about gaining the yardage, so I don't lose my spot."

Fair enough. Wouldn't we all, in that same situation, be concerned? But I knew all she needed to do was shift her intention. I asked my client to focus on imagining the kick itself. Imagine where her body and head placement should be to achieve optimal distance. After discussing the details, we practiced repeatedly on the field. When she kicked with intention, focusing on the physical details, she picked up four or five yards just like that. The focus shifted to the actual process, dispelling concern about staying on the team.

Have you ever watched the video of Ben Hogan's slow-motion golf swing at Seminole Golf Club in Florida? Look it up on You Tube (https://www.you-tube.com/watch?v=p56EGLiKnBA). Notice how he was able to slow down his swing himself to look as though it was slow motion. His ability to swing with such intent and know every nuance of his own swing demonstrates the high level of focus he possessed. When he swung on the course, his mind was on the movement of his club, not the ball. The intention drove his attention and synergy was achieved as it was with my client, the soccer player.

Additionally, when an athlete isn't at practice or competing, they should practice awareness throughout the day. Like we did previously, have your child think of a room, and ask them what they saw. Then ask them to sweep it in their mind again but identifying something they missed the first time. This may seem super simple, but it will train their brain. The more your athlete practices being hyper focused, the more their self-awareness increases. More importantly, this skill naturally transfers to the playing field and everywhere else in their lives.

An important question is: How does the athlete do it all? How do they focus on the physical execution and stay tuned into what's happening all around them? I have had clients who say, "Well if I'm thinking about where my opponents are, how will I still execute the kick [for example] properly?" In order to understand this concept, I must explain the difference between the conscious and the subconscious mind.

The conscious mind is where new information is processed and learned. For example, when you learn to drive a car, you are consciously aware of where your hands and feet are and what you're looking at. The task is all new and it's being processed into your conscious mind. Once that task is embedded and its learned, the subconscious mind takes over. The subconscious mind is more automatic than the conscious mind—think of it as your own personal autopilot. When you get into your car, you are no longer thinking about where each body part is or which foot to use where.

I gamble to say there are many times when you get in and drive while your conscious mind is processing an idea that has nothing to do with driving. How many times have you arrived at your destination and can't remember the specifics of how you got there? That's because your subconscious drove the car, not your conscious, which was probably processing another thought or idea.

Just like the example of driving a car, the subconscious mind takes over in sports. Once your body has learned and mastered a movement, it fires it off without you thinking about it, allowing your conscious mind to be aware of what's happening around it. This will be important to understand as we talk about attentional shifting and imaging below.

Attentional Shifting

When increasing one's awareness of their environment, there comes into play a skill called attentional shifting. This particular skill takes focus and awareness to the next level. It gives the athlete the ability to change or shift their attention during play. Now for some sports, like racecar driving, football, or hockey, this is done at a very fast pace.

Let's look at it first from a sport that isn't moving at warp speed—golf—to better understand the concept. In the game of golf, you first assess where you want the ball to go. Then you can determine how you want to shape the shot, how you're lined up, or where you should place the ball in your stance. Once you take your stance, your attention is no longer on the target but on what you are going to do with the club. Your focus now must be on the technical components of the swing. This entire thought process is an example of attentional shifting.

Try out this concept right now. Focus on one thing in the room you are sitting in. Without moving your eyes, find an object on your right. Now again, without moving your eyes, find an object on your left. Did you lose your awareness of the object on your right? I bet you did. This is attentional shifting.

How does an athlete practice this? They would do the same exercise you just did, and it would be done daily in order to increase their attentional focus. Not unlike with imagery, the more you do this simple exercise off the field, the more embedded the skill will become, and the more they'll be able to use it when they need it the most.

Why is that important? Well, Wayne Gretzky has said that, "It's not important where the puck is but where the puck is going-" (Kirby, 2014).

As a hockey player, because of the speed of the game, it's important to think one step ahead to where the puck will be next. This requires incredibly fast attentional shifting.

The speed at which an athlete will need to use this skill will depend on the sport they are playing, but intense focus and ability to shift awareness around is crucial for all athletic endeavors.

Imagery

Practice and repetition are essential to improve both physical and mental performance. In addition to seeing things with intention and having the ability to shift their attention, your athlete needs to practice creating scenarios in their mind that could potentially happen on the playing field. They need to imagine realistic scenarios that could occur during play and how they should react to them.

When your athlete imagines their performance in a game, they should imagine it in three different ways: what their body will feel, what they will look like from afar, and how they'll see it themselves. To deepen your understanding, let's look at this concept as if your athlete is a soccer goalie. You would have your goalie imagine how they will kick the ball down field to their teammate. Step one will be for the goalie to imagine how the kick will physically feel: what will their muscles feel like, what will their body experience as they execute the kick. Next, the athlete will imagine what that kick will look like from a distance, as if they were watching themselves on TV. And finally, they will imagine the action from a first-person perspective: how the kick will look from their own eyes and what their eyes will see happening as the kicked ball goes down the field.

These three separate variations are part of the process called Imagery. The individual visualizations are known as proprioception, internal visualization, and external visualization. Proprioception is the felt experience without moving the body. It is a conscious awareness of the body's movement in space without the body actually moving. External visualization is how the athlete sees themselves from the third person perspective. And the internal visualization is what the athlete sees when the action is taking place.

The reason I have my clients use imagery during practice is to have them train their mind to replace negative thoughts such as fear or anxiety with a more productive and supportive focus on a specific action.

Back to my soccer client, who was attempting to gain yardage. Before we talked, when she kicked, her intentions centered on whether or not she could or couldn't produce the additional yardage. I asked her to change her intention and to kick with her mind on mechanics. We used the three points of imagery to achieve this goal. I asked her to imagine the kick in her mind: how it would feel and how it would look from her perception—proprioception (felt experience) and internal visualization. Once she physically made the kick, her intentions were on the physical aspects of the kick, and since she imagined it, her muscles fired off in real time.

This entire practice centered around removing the athlete's "feelings" when she kicked and replacing them with an instructional approach to *how* she kicked. Her brain didn't focus on "what happens if I don't make it." Now it focused on the physical aspects of the kick. Once that occurred, her muscles took over and she gained the necessary yardage. The skills were always there, but her mind had previously blocked her from achieving the goal. This simple shift in her thought process removed that block. This exercise goes hand in hand with building self-efficacy (See chapter on self-efficacy).

When an athlete removes how they "feel" about the action they need to perform, and instead focuses on what they have to "do" to perform it correctly, the action they desire is almost always achieved.

I work with many gymnasts. Even at the Olympic level, it's not uncommon for them to be unable to perform a task they've done a million times. About 70% of gymnasts form mental blocks at some point during their career (Feigley, 2006).

One gymnast I work with could not perform a backhand spring into a layout on the balance beam. However, she was about to make the national team and was expected to perform this move at the USA Gymnastics training camp. Clearly the stakes were high.

Over the phone, she and I discussed the mechanics of the move, specifically what she was thinking when she did it. Not unlike the soccer player, she was focused on what she felt at the time, not what she needed to do.

We began with some imagery: proprioception, internal, and external visualization. Then I asked her what she thought about while performing the layout. She indicated the hand placement felt weird to her. When she went from the back handspring to the layout, her hands moved away from her body. That hand movement threw her off. It "felt weird" to her. That movement was the trigger point where she tensed and, in turn, was unable to complete the move.

The solution? I told her that, at the moment she moves her hands away from herself, she should immediately imagine her body relaxing. Sounds simple and probably silly to some, but at that point in the move, she changed her focus. The focus went from "feeling weird" to instructionally relaxing her muscles. That change in focus solved the issue almost immediately.

Three days after we spoke, she had to perform this series of moves at the Olympic training facility. Immediately upon arrival, the director, aware of her struggles, put her on the balance beam to perform those moves, three times in a row. She did it and made the national team.

Mental Prompts

Another critical imaging technique that can assist the player struggling with negative thoughts is the use of mental prompts. This is where the player identifies his or her negative thoughts at the time the mistake is made. What were they thinking before they struck out, or failed to catch the lacrosse pass? It's at that point that the player must immediately replace the negative thought with a positive image.

Here's why it works: The brain cannot simultaneously hold a negative thought and a positive image at the same time. Mental prompts train your brain to replace negative thoughts with positive images. The process for this to work is identifying the triggers—the points at which the negative thoughts enter the mind.

I work with a young competitive golfer who is probably the most talented junior golfer I've seen. After being invited to play at the prestigious Carey Cup, he shot a horrific 92 for one of his rounds, pulling him out of the competition. He described to me his negative thoughts prior to hitting his shots. He kept worrying that he would keep hitting a "block" —a.k.a. hit it to the right. He subconsciously attempted to avoid doing that, which only produced fear.

I explained to him the use of mental prompts. Before he made any shot and a negative thought entered his head, he immediately had to replace it with a positive image. For him that positive image was a "good shot." However, the positive image can be whatever the player wants. It can be a picture, a memory, time with friends, or any other positive thought. The important thing is to use the prompts repetitively to train the brain, so that when a negative thought enters the mind, it automatically replaces it with the positive image. The final result is that the body relaxes, and the error is avoided.

In the case of the young golfer, he trained his mind and brain over the next few rounds and happily reported back to me that in subsequent events, his scores were back in line and that he had utilized the mental prompts effectively.

This is good in golf where time before each shot allows this training of the brain. However, in a fast-moving team sport like basketball, soccer, or hockey, for example, a player does not have the luxury of time. Yet, mental prompts are just as effective in these sports as well. The training is just different.

Instead of occurring during a game or practice, mental prompt training happens off the field. The player, in their mind, places themselves at their trigger point when the negative thought occurs and immediately replaces it with a positive image. This is done multiple times throughout the day for as many days as it takes to be embedded. Again, the positive image can be anything.

This technique of replacing negative thoughts with a positive image was developed in the 1950's by Temple University professor Joseph Wolpe. He developed the therapy based on reciprocal inhibition. Reciprocal inhibition states that "different psychological responses are incompatible with each other-" (Wolpe, 1968). In non-scientific terms, this describes the fact that your brain cannot hold a negative thought and a positive thought at the same time. In the past, this therapy was primarily used with phobias and anxiety. Yet with athletes, it's been utilized effectively in reversing negative thoughts or anxiety during performance.

In addition to positive images used in mental prompting, a player can also use certain words as triggers to remove the negativity or anxiety. Typically, I recommend words that evoke a physical feeling and are instructionally based— words that make you think of an action—such as "smooth" or "flow". We do not want to confuse imaging with feelings in an emotional sense. Emotions have nothing to do with these techniques. We are trying to conjure a certain physical feeling to embed in our brain, so the muscles respond on demand. Emotions are performance killers, as we will discuss in our chapter on self-efficacy.

For example, I have a golfer who participates in long drive competitions. He does quite well in these competitions, but he was looking to improve his swing. Since he is also a painter, I asked him how his preferred swing would look if he painted it. He replied, "Smooth." I directed him to imagine painting his swing in his mind and then, to utter the word "smooth" in his mind before he swings.

He practiced this exercise every time he stood over the ball and it literally over time changed his swing to the way he wanted it. Now every time he stands over the ball and says the word "smooth" in his mind, he automatically imagines the painting.

Mental prompting is also very effective in sports that involve grips, such as golf, tennis, paddle tennis, or baseball. Many parents and coaches complain that their athlete holds the grip far too tightly, negatively impacting their swing. Instructionally, these players, at the point the grip takes place, implant a positive image in their mind. This mental prompt relaxes the grip. The trigger for the image becomes the initial gripping of the equipment. Only with practice and repetition will mental prompts be embedded and become automatic.

What Happens If It No Longer Works?

For all of the imaging techniques I just discussed, it's not unusual for the player, their parents, or coaches to ask, "What happens if this stops working?" I tell them, "It may, and if it does, we'll do it all over again but change the imagery." If the player once used the word "smooth" to enact a positive image but it stops working, we will find another word that works for them. This process is iterative. Nothing is permanent because athletes are always growing and changing, so too does their mental game. However, the process and proven techniques can be used effectively time and time again.

Hypnosis

Pro golfer Phil Mickelson once said, "Mental rehearsal is just as important as physical rehearsal-" (Mackenzie, 2009). Phil, like many other professional athletes, reaps the benefits of a strong mental game. In fact, it's been long reported that Mickelson, along with Tiger Woods, have worked with sport psychologists. And in training with a mental coach, both have been reported to have used hypnosis as part of their therapy (Fogg, 2009). Hypnosis is a tool that can help an athlete achieve greater focus and reduce anxiety to give them the mental edge in competition.

Quite often, individuals misunderstand hypnosis. As with anything not widely understood, there is a fear. A common fear is the notion that you are surrendering your mind to someone else, that somehow, the hypnotist can alter who you are as a person, which is not the case. In hypnosis, you cannot change someone's values or alter who they are down deep.

Hypnosis is an altered state of consciousness used to influence performance or relax the mind and body (Lazarus, 2013). Hypnosis is a tool I use with clients whose negative thoughts or perhaps phobias are severe and with clients looking to enhance focus.

A hypnotic state is natural, in fact during certain points of a human's sleep pattern, they are in a hypnogogic state (Bell, 2016). In the hypnogogic state, the individual is not truly asleep, but in a trance-like state. Oftentimes if a dream occurs during this state, an individual can awake feeling like it actually happened. In truth, the experience did occur for them—not in reality, but in their subconscious (Bell, 2016).

How does this help with an athlete's mental game? In one case, I worked with a high jumper who needed to gain distance. She knew she had to hold her head a certain way when she jumped to achieve maximum distance, but she was riddled with negative thoughts that stopped her from making her best jump. In hypnosis, we trained her brain to replace those negative thoughts immediately with a positive image, inducing a relaxed and focused state. She was then able to focus on her head placement and perform a successful jump.

If you believe your athlete would benefit from hypnosis or you want to learn more, please seek out a licensed professional to ensure you are getting the appropriate care. Hypnosis is not a licensed act, so not all hypnotists are a licensed psychologist.

CHAPTER 6

Self-Efficacy vs. Confidence

Here's the scene: You pull into the parking spot next to the field, put the car in park, and glance at your athlete. "Let's go!" you declare as enthusiastically as possible on minimum caffeine.

"Yep!" Your superstar yells as he races out of the car.

But by the time you've popped open your folding chair, your kid is running back toward you, "Did you see the other team? They're huge! We're done for!"

You give the adult, mature parent speech, the one your dad gave you: "You go out there and play your game. You don't need to be the biggest guy out there. All you need is confidence!" You make sure to inflect a sense of authority in your voice to drive home your point.

Your athlete looks at you, shakes his head with that deer-in-headlights stare, and runs back to the field.

Another parent unfolds his chair next to you, sits down and says, "I heard this team is undefeated and by the looks of them, we're going to be eaten alive!"

"Nah," you answer, "Our guys just need a little confidence!"

The guy nods as his kid runs over to him and says almost word for word what yours just uttered. The dad responds, "Just be confident! Don't let them intimidate you!"

Again, the young athlete shakes his head with the same blank look and runs back on the field. You and the other parent share a knowing look and a sense of having done your job, teaching them the importance of being confident.

After your team loses the game, you spill out some sage advice to preserve any level of confidence your player has left. "You win some and you lose some. You'll get them next week. Shake this loss off."

Your athlete nods in agreement but you see his confidence has taken a blow along with the rest of the team's. You think to yourself, *Just let them win next week so they can gain their confidence back.*

Whether your child plays a team sport or an individual one, the knee jerk reaction, when self-doubt looms, is to give them the "old confidence" speech. We wait for them to give us the sign they understand, but realistically, we know they are one failed shot, catch, kick, or movement away from having self-doubt creep back in.

Like any parent, I constantly preached the need for confidence, for my child to believe in himself during his golf competitions. However, despite the times he proclaimed confidence, every missed shot chipped away at him, destroying his belief in himself and ultimately landing him short of his desired finish. Even more puzzling were the times when his confidence was visibly low and he came home holding a first-place trophy. I chalked it up to a scattering of anomalies until Dr. Nick explained a very crucial fact: confidence is not a predictor of performance.

Dr. Nick

Parents and coaches bring athletes to me when their performance falls below their ability level. In our initial conversation, the adults will almost always say the athlete's performance is a direct result of low confidence. "We need you to help build their confidence so they can perform at their highest level," they'll say. Given that most adults have been led to believe in a one-to-one correlation between performance and confidence, I know changing this notion will be my first hurdle.

My initial question is this: "If he or she has low or no confidence, and if what they need to win is confidence, how will they get it?"

The parent or coach usually replies, "Once he or she starts winning their confidence will go up and then more wins will follow."

"Well, if the confidence is low, and you believe confidence is the predictor of performance, then how will he or she ever win to get more confident?"

I continue by explaining that we can't hope for a win or put athletes in situations where they will easily win just to boost their confidence. Say you place the athlete in situations where an easy win is inevitable, and they win a few times. Their confidence appears to rise. But then something happens, and they are faced with a challenge and fail to meet a goal or simply don't perform as well as they had previously. Now the athlete has experienced some amount of defeat, their confidence inevitably takes a blow and doubt seeps in, eventually ruling their performance again. Confidence, despite what we have been led to believe, is not what athlete's need to improve their performance.

Confidence is a belief or feeling that you have certain abilities. Yet, beliefs can allow for doubt. Doubt is the great destroyer of the athlete's mental game. An athlete can believe they can do well, but belief always leaves the door open for doubt to enter. The mind easily replaces positive feelings with negative all the time. It only takes one second of doubt for your athlete to start fighting negative thoughts when they should be focused on the specifics of their performance.

If confidence isn't the answer, what is? Self-efficacy. Self-efficacy should be the ultimate goal for your athlete.

Self-efficacy, under my definition, is separate and distinct from confidence. Self-efficacy is *not* a feeling or belief. It is the truth about one's ability to perform a skill. This truth or knowledge is based on trust, and it's developed over time as a result of dedicated practice. The self-efficacious athlete has developed trust, derived from proof, in their physical skill set. Their ability to perform with consistency over time, during practice, and in competition, is the proof that manifests the trust and faith in their abilities. These athletes don't think, feel or believe they can do it. They know they can.

There are things we do every day in which we demonstrate self-efficacy. When you head to your car, do you stop and wonder if you know how to operate it? When you sit behind the wheel, do you tell yourself to have confidence, to believe you can drive? Of course not. I guarantee you never even question that skill. You know you can operate your vehicle because you've proven it.

Now remember back to the first day you got your license. How different do you feel now versus then? I bet pretty different. Perhaps, along with excitement, there was a sprinkling of apprehension. It wasn't until you proved your skill to yourself over time and with constant repetition that you can now be self-efficacious about operating your car.

Imagine your athlete never questioning their ability to perform on the course, field, court, or wherever they play and just focusing on playing the game. Game changer? Yes, absolutely. Let's look at some examples of self-efficacious athletes.

In 2000, at the Bell Canadian Open, Tiger Woods made an incredible shot—probably the best of his career, if not one of the most memorable (Mitrosilis, 2009). On the 18th hole at Glenn Abby his tee shot ended up in the fairway bunker. Faced with 213 yards, and a water hazard to get over, most professional golfers would have laid-up, playing it safe. Not Tiger. With a 6 iron in hand, he hit the ball out of the bunker, over the water, and landed it on the back of the green. In true Tiger form, he made the putt and delivered the win. In fact, 2000 was the year he won all three opens: Canadian, U.S., and British.

In 2002, at the PGA Championship, Tiger's tee shot ended up in the fairway bunker with a downhill lie. A tree directly in front of him, he took a 3 iron, hooked the shot out of the bunker and around the tree, and he landed it eight feet from the hole.

In 2012, at the Memorial Tournament at Muirfield Village, Tiger landed his ball in the rough, 50 feet from the pin. A chip could cause the ball to roll down the hill and land in the water hazard. Did Tiger flinch? No, he hit a flop shot perfectly, and the ball rolled right into the hole (Mitrosilis, 2009).

Tiger's career has been riddled with moments like these and the list is too voluminous to go through completely. This is why, as spectators, we are in awe of his ability to pull off the impossible shot so effortlessly, as if it was no major feat. Yet, it wasn't that every shot he made was perfect: otherwise he would never end up in these situations. It was his ability to get out of these predicaments with such skill and poise that has captivated a world of golfers and non-golfers alike.

What makes Tiger so good at getting out of those situations? The majority of spectators might claim its Tiger's confidence around his abilities that allow for his execution of the "impossible shots." I am not among the majority. Confidence is not why Tiger has excelled on the course. What has made Tiger excel is self-efficacy; he knows the truth of his own capabilities.

What do you think of when you hear the name Michael Phelps? Great American swimmer, superior athlete, 28 Olympic gold medals? At any time when you hear the name Michael Phelps do you envision a man who lacks confidence or is anxious? No, I would guess not.

However, Phelps has spoken out about being riddled with anxiety and depression (Shaffer, 2018). His belief system does not mimic what society thinks of when we envision an Olympic athlete, especially one so decorated. But despite his internal emotional struggles, Michael has still achieved untold success. How? Because his confidence levels had no impact on his performance. How he *felt* had little consequence on his ability to swim and compete. His truth, his self-efficacy, is what propelled him to win all those medals. For Michael, his truth or knowledge of his ability to perform in the pool never wavered despite all his anxiety or negative feelings about himself.

Phelps was quoted as saying about winning the medals, "I think that part is pretty easy—it's hard work, dedication, not giving up-" (Scutti, 2018). That part was indeed easy because he had proven to himself, through intense practice and dedication, the truth about his abilities. He didn't feel he was good enough to win; he *knew* he could win. Phelps knew he physically could get to the finish faster than anyone else. Phelps held his own truth about his skills, a fact no different than rain is wet or the sun is hot.

Despite his inner conflicts, the one truth Phelps held was that he was physically capable. In the water, at the point of performance in competition, his mind was keenly focused on a specific task: what he physically had to do to win the race (Svrluga, 2008). Combining truth and focus on specific physical skills in executing a performance is what self-efficacious athletes do that sets them apart. They don't wonder how they feel or what they believe at that critical moment of execution, just what they technically must do and what they *can* do.

Skeptics may claim Phelps was confident in his ability to swim even if his confidence in himself was low. But that's not the case. Confidence is rooted in feelings; it's an emotion. Self-efficacy is rooted in truth, based on facts. Michael Phelps didn't think he could do it; he knew without any doubt. His truth developed—like Tiger's did—from dedicated practice and perseverance over time. And during those moments of performance, Tiger and Phelps were not contemplating how they felt or what they believed. They were focused on the specifics of the performance. They never needed to question their abilities; they already knew the answer.

Perhaps the thought, *This is a nice concept, but I don't really see the difference and neither will my player,* has popped into your head. The concept of self-efficacy may seem too vague to apply in practical terms on the field, course, or court for your player. But before you ignore it, let me explain how this works in practical terms with the players I coach.

First, remember a key fact about the mind: The mind cannot process a negative and a positive feeling at the same time (Garavan, 1998; McElree, 1998). It's been proven that among the thousands of thoughts running through our minds each day, up to 70% are negative (Raghunathan, 2013), which tells us that negative feelings typically rule over positive ones. How many times have we heard someone say, "It's easier to believe the negative things about myself than the positive." Therefore, you can understand why I insist my athletes stop focusing on feelings. Negative feelings will derail a performance in a second. In self-efficacy, the athlete's mind is focused on facts and truths, not feelings.

I had a client, a collegiate lacrosse player, who was up for Player of the Year in his conference but was in danger of not achieving it. When I initially assessed him, his confidence scores were quite low, meaning he doubted his ability to perform at his highest level. His coach wanted those confidence scores to increase. But I knew his confidence scores didn't matter. This player needed to change his thought process on the playing field.

I spoke with the player in my office for one hour. During that session we focused on one simple question, "Can you do x, y, and z? Yes or no. I don't want to know how you *feel* about it. I want to know one thing: can you do it? Can you physically make x, y, and z happen in a game? Think about the specifics, the mechanics of your performance, and whether or not you can do it before you answer." He thought and then answered a definitive, *yes.*

"Ok, good. Then at the moment you're on the field, I want your mind on the specifics of what you need to do." With his mind focused on the moves he needed to make and knowing he could make them, it precluded any negative feelings or beliefs from happening in his mind.

The lacrosse player finished his season and won Player of the Year after that session. That shift in thinking, of focusing on knowledge instead of his feelings during his time on the field, allowed him to do what he was physically capable of. The doubt was no longer in his mind; the truth was. We replaced his negative feelings with proven truths.

Two other clients, both high jumpers, had the same discussion around self-efficacy with me. I posed the same question to each of them, "Can you do it? I don't care how you *feel* about it. Self-efficacy is *not* a feeling; it's a truth. *Can* you do it?" One jumper answered yes, the other didn't know.

So, we broke the mechanics of their jumps down into physical specifics: head placement, feet placement, and so on. I re-asked the same question for each technical movement necessary to execute the desired jump, "Can you place your head this way and execute the jump?" This time both their answers were an absolute *yes*. Remember, this is not an emotional process. Move away from how the athlete feels about it and move toward the truth about specific physical competencies. Extricating negative feelings produces laser-like focus, leaving no place for doubt to exist. The player is then able to perform at the desired level.

In the case of the high jumpers, they each picked up over two inches right away.

Understand, the lacrosse player and the high jumpers had spent countless hours of practice dedicated to honing their skills, so at the point of our sessions they knew what their capabilities were. They just needed to shift their thought process when executing a performance.

In the case of very young athletes, we can and should start working toward self-efficacy. They may not be old enough to assess their skill levels or even have enough to pull from to form a truth, but when they are playing, it's up to parents and coaches to not focus on feelings. Don't focus on them thinking they can or cannot kick a ball down the field or catch a grounder. Tell them to do their best and to remember what they were taught in practice. Make sure that you communicate that a missed shot or catch is just something to learn from. Be positive but specific in your feedback. Feelings should only enter the conversation when you exit the field and you ask if they had fun.

Why Is Self-Efficacy Better Than Confidence?

A friend told me a story about a middle school lacrosse player who wanted desperately to play the goalie position. He loved the position. He had a passion for it, yet he began missing shots taken on his goal with increasing frequency. His team's anxiety grew every time he stepped into the goal and so did his.

Before one game, his coaches warmed him up and he caught every shot. Yet, when they sent him in to play, inevitably the parting words were "You can do this, you just need to have confidence." Those last thoughts were telling the player how he should feel, and negative feelings can override positive very quickly. Now, the goalie may have run on the field feeling good, but as the game progressed, he started to battle his fears of missing the ball.

What made the difference for this lacrosse player happened after an especially difficult loss. His mother asked an assistant coach to work on specific movements and shots with the player to build his confidence, because isn't that what he needed? Of course, by now you know my answer is no to needing confidence, but yes, he did need some guidance.

The young assistant coach began working with him outside of general practice sessions and broke down the moves and skills needed to catch any potential shot. This coach never addressed feelings or discussed the need for confidence; he stuck to the facts of the athlete's abilities. Determination, dedication, and repetition engrained proof of the player's skill set to the player himself. During these practice sessions, the coach kept telling the player to focus on where he stood, where the other players were, what he needed to tell his defense men in front of him, his stick placement, and other skills and strategies. They focused on specifics and practiced all possible scenarios. They used deep, dedicated practice to build a truth around the goalie's abilities (discussed in further detail in our chapter on practice).

When he returned as goalie, the player focused on executing the skills he knew he had in order to stop the ball. Feelings were less and less of a factor in his mind with each game. When the ball was shot at him, he was thinking about the specific skills he needed to use to accomplish his goals, not his feelings about whether he could or could not stop the ball. In time, he shut out the competition on a regular basis.

The chapter on practice provided more specific details on how to structure practices for your athletes to make them more effective in fostering an athlete's truth, rather than building feelings of confidence. So, refer back to it when structuring an athlete's practice, and keep feelings out of the picture.

How to Instill Self-Efficacy

Renowned psychologist Albert Bandura contributed significantly to psychology's understanding of self-efficacy. Bandura defined self-efficacy as, "… the belief in one's ability to influence events that affect one's life and control over the way these events are experienced-" (Buchanan, 2016). He uses the word "belief" in his definition, but I want to be clear: beliefs exist with or without the presence of doubt. Bandura is referring to a belief without doubt based on proof or, as I refer to it, faith. Bandura also makes it very clear that self-efficacy is something anyone can achieve, no matter what their environment or past. Bandura lays out four, specific ways an individual builds self-efficacy: mastery experiences, social modeling, social persuasion, and states of physiology (Buchanan, 2016).

Mastery is referring to the establishment and integration of trust and faith in one's skill set through practice—as discussed previously (Buchanan, 2016). Trust can be defined as a belief in the truth about someone or something (Merriam-Webster dictionary, n.d.). But beliefs can be based on falsehoods, and they can allow for doubt. Under this definition, you can trust another person's word and still have some amount of doubt. The only way to eliminate potential doubt is to gain trust based on proof. Proof is achieved through practice; a more concrete scientific approach. Trust based on proof is the definition I use for self-efficacy.

The second part of mastery is faith. Faith is defined as a complete trust in someone or something (Merriam-Webster dictionary, n.d.). My definition, as it pertains to self-efficacy, is that faith is a belief, without doubt, and future orientated. Future orientated pertains to something the athlete hasn't experienced yet. The execution is the same, but the external factors are new.

It is the integration of trust and faith, under my definitions, that leads an athlete to being self-efficacious. The athlete with trust and faith never doubts their abilities because they are based on proof, dispelling any doubt and are future orientated.

For example, I have an athlete who plays golf for an NCAA Division I college, and in his freshman year, won his first competition with a score of 65. A huge accomplishment. The physical process of playing golf was the same, but this player had never experienced playing in a collegiate environment. For many new collegiate players, in any sport, this can be quite daunting. However, my athlete had known he could go into this new situation successfully and had trust, based on proof in his skill set. In other words, he possessed self-efficacy.

Another way to get your athlete to develop self-efficacy is through social modeling and social persuasion (Buchanan, 2016). Social modeling and social persuasion are about having the right role model and mentor; sometimes this could be one person or several individuals. While choosing a role model and/or mentor, the athlete must demonstrate self-efficacy. Albert Bandura stated, "It is essential to have a mentor that is knowledgeable and practices what they preach-" (Buchanan, 2016).

Parents and coaches can guide their child's selection of a role model through discussions about famous or non-famous athletes that demonstrate the characteristics of self-efficacy. Let's say you're watching an athlete on television and your athlete thinks they are amazing. Take the opportunity to ask questions: "Why do you think they are so good at what they do? How do you think they can perform so well under such intense pressure? Do you think they have good qualities as a role model and why?" Start the conversation.

Another critical step in establishing an environment that promotes self-efficacy is for parents and coaches alike to use the right language when critiquing their athlete's performance (Buchanan, 2016). Go back to the words and language we discussed in previous chapters on Mindset and Grit to refresh your memory on specific language. Words should be growth orientated, truthful, and specific. Generalities, such as "You did amazing today," or "You're such a great player," or "You fell apart today! Way to lose it for the team!" These statements will not foster self-efficacy. Instead, comments or critiques should be specific: "I liked the way you anticipated every shot and got in front of the ball," or "Your hand position on the stick today was not solid throughout the game, causing you to drop the ball. So, work on keeping your hand placement consistent and you will avoid those drops."

What Are the Benefits of Self-Efficacy?

There are significant benefits to having your athlete develop self-efficacy beyond them performing at their best. As with all the attributes addressed in this book, the benefits are far reaching, much beyond sport. Yet sport is the perfect vehicle to cultivate them. Psychologist Albert Bandura said there are four types of potential benefits that your athlete will develop as a byproduct of self-efficacy: cognitive, motivational, emotional, and decisional (Buchanan, 2016).

The cognitive benefit is the ability to see oneself as one's driver for change. The self-efficacious athlete will understand that their efforts will get them to their goals. So, as they establish new milestones, they will know with hard work and determination that they have the power within them to make it happen.

The motivational benefit is that the athlete sees an obstacle or a roadblock as just something to overcome, not a deal breaker to their desire for a specific outcome.

The emotional benefit of self-efficacy is seeing negative emotions as part of being human and not debilitating. Emotional challenges are seen the same as any other challenge and just another thing they know they will overcome and be better for having done it.

Finally, the decisional benefit is that the athlete drives his or her own bus, so to speak. These individuals know themselves and they use truths about themselves to make changes or decisions that will impact their game positively (Buchanan, 2016).

Despite all the benefits of self-efficacy, Bandura warns there are two things that could potentially derail an athlete from the path to self-efficacy: easily achieving success or experiencing overwhelming failure (Buchanan, 2016). Both these experiences could damage the development of self-efficacy. Self-efficacy must be obtained through hard work and dedication. Only through hard work can the athlete acknowledge the truth about their abilities—not through the easy win. And, if the hard work is present but the goals are far beyond the realistic reach of the athlete, the athlete may lose motivation or passion to work hard in the future.

Why Positive Feedback Doesn't Work

Neither confidence nor self-efficacy come from constant positive feedback. As we discussed previously, critiques of a player's performance should be constructive and pointed. The critique should focus on specifics. When we try to "talk a player up" to instill a positive attitude, it's in generalities. The information is not useful, nor does it create teaching moments, but it gives the player a false sense of how good they are and what skills they currently possess.

Countless times I've heard an encouraging parent trying get their baseball player, for example, to relax and pitch better on the mound. Before the game they tell him: "You are so good at pitching! Go out there and pitch us a no-hitter!" What are the effects of those words? Will the pitcher perform leaps and bounds better than usual because his parent said he would? No, the words did nothing but potentially create expectations in the players mind. These expectations could be anxiety producing, which can allow for positive thoughts to be replaced by negative thoughts almost immediately.

You will never change your child's perception of their abilities by making up false positives or embellishing their abilities. It's a waste of time and counterproductive. Just stop. Instead, give repeated, specific feedback with a focus on being growth-minded, to foster faith and trust, creating building blocks toward self-efficacy.

If all Tiger Woods' dad did was tell him how great he was, do you think that when he hit an errant shot, he would have the self-efficacy to hit the next shot well? If you are told how wonderful you are and never told specifically what you do right and what you need to improve, you will have a hard time with failure. You will fall apart when things don't go your way. Remember, psychologist Albert Bandura warns against success that is too easily obtained. Dedication and determination, which include times of failure, must be the vehicles to learning the athlete's truth (Buchanan, 2016).

Failure's Impact of Self-Efficacy

Failure is defined as not meeting a goal or expectation. Everyone fails. No one has ever gotten 100% on everything. To err is human, as they say. Coaches, parents, and teachers need to understand this concept. Oftentimes when I am explaining self-efficacy to a parent, their response is, "So, if they learn to have self-efficacy, they won't ever play badly?"

Immediately I respond, "Of course not. Everyone has moments of failure or bad performance. That is called being human. The difference is an athlete with self-efficacy sees failure as part of life and something to learn from." You can have self-efficacy, but with self-efficacy comes the additional understanding that if you fail, you don't lose that faith. The athlete accepts that he or she has made an error and moves on.

Tiger knew his truth: that he could hit the ball and make it go how he envisioned it. He also knew that hitting a bad shot just meant he was human and that nothing is 100% a 100% of the time. That is why he was able to hit the next shot to get him where he needed to be. He lived his truth, void of fear and doubt.

Can self-efficacy get your athlete where they need to be all by itself? No. And just like with grit, self-efficacy relies upon other factors. The presence of a growth-mindset, grit, goal setting, and dedicated practice are all crucial to the development of self-efficacy. Again, each attribute we discuss builds on the other and is dependent on the other in order to exist.

CHAPTER 7

Assessing Readiness

Quietly seated in the back of a library full of mothers wearing the same shoes, clothes, and sunglasses perched on top of their heads, I listened excitedly to my son's future kindergarten teachers. As they happily rattled off the upcoming year's activities, I pondered how he would take to it all. Enter the school's interim principal: an older man with a soft demeanor and a sweet gentle face. He reiterated the teachers' sweet sentiments of the exciting year of learning our children were about to have. Then to the homogenized group of moms he said, "Most of you have high expectations, but as a dad and grandfather, I have to be honest and say that for most of you in here, your children will be average and that's not only ok, it's a good thing."

The inaudible gasps shook the room harder than a 4.0 earthquake. The sugary sweet smiles turned flat as if they had been licking a lollipop and someone had ripped it from their hands. Sweetness and light fell to irritation and disbelief. I was no exception. My child walked at nine and a half months, he spoke full sentences at a year, and he could argue his point better than Johnny Cochran—to me there was no way he was average. A quiet internal conversation reverberated in my head and I'm pretty sure, given the crowd, I wasn't alone.

We have become a society devoted to distinguishing our kids in academics and athletics. We push our kids to be the best at everything, most notably sports. But what is the cost of an environment focused on achieving perfection? Who will end up paying the bill: your athlete?

Dr. Nick

Youth sports have evolved into an institution since they began in the early 1900s (Friedman, 2013). Some argue that the mandate for school attendance became the impetus of youth sports. States requiring children to attend school created structure around their days and free time became identifiable. Parents wanted to fill that free time, and youth sports emerged as a way to achieve that.

Youth programs started with Pop Warner football in 1929, followed by Little League baseball in 1939. Suddenly children were participating in organized sports across the nation, in addition to backyard or street pick-up games. By the 1960s, youth sports became a family pastime, with parents toting their kids to practice and games for sports like baseball, basketball, hockey, and football.

Eventually, parents began connecting sports with college entrance and the push for children to play sports at the collegiate level began. The realization that sports meant easier admission to higher-level institutions created a more competitive environment among youth athletics (Friedman, 2013).

By the 1990s and into the 2000s, the competition ramped up considerably with the added push for scholarship money. According to The Aspen Institute, the amount of money given to Division I and II schools has gone from approximately $500 million in the 1990s to somewhere around $2.7 billion as of 2016 (MacDonald, 2016). The availability of scholarship money, rising cost of tuition, and increased competition over college admissions have incited many parents to push their kids to play collegiate athletics.

As a sport psychologist, I have seen an increase in clients for this reason alone. However, we must remember, oftentimes the desires and motives of an athlete's parents do not always correlate with the athlete's desires and motives. In fact, many of my clients have parents whose desires are different from their own. These situations create family strife, anxiety, and resentment.

Specialization

What does my mini history lesson have to do with specialization and child readiness? We need to understand how we got to this place with youth sports to understand the dynamics behind the push to specialize. Understand that motivational factors for kids in sports, at elite levels at such early ages—more than ever before—is directly affected by the desire for collegiate athletic participation and scholarships.

So, with the carrots of college admissions and scholarship money dangling in the faces of today's parents, early specialization is on the rise. Specialization is when an athlete focuses on one sport to practice and play year-round. Young athletes are specializing earlier and with higher frequency with the intent to create elite athletes. But, there are flaws in that thinking. In fact, there are serious physical and psychological risks associated with early specialization.

In 2016, NCAA President Mark Emmert stated in an interview with The Aspen Institute Sports & Society program, "[Student-athletes] are coming into college now with so much more experience than a typical high school kid would have, because they have been playing quarterback 12 months out the year, they have been going to summer camp, they've been going to an IMG academy [a preparatory boarding school and sports training institution]-" (MacDonald, 2016). Emmert goes on to say that with all this focus on pushing an athlete to perform, the athlete as a person is overlooked and that physical injuries have increased significantly in severity and quantity (MacDonald, 2016).

So again, what does all this mean for a parent deciphering whether his or her child is ready for specialization or higher-level competition? Let me ask you this: How did you know your child was ready for anything in their toddler years? Whether it was to eat finger foods or to walk or to play in the sandbox, I bet most of you would say, "Well, I kind of just knew by my child's actions." And a handful of you would say, "I knew he/she was ready because my pediatrician said so."

Both are correct ways to understand a child's readiness. Some amount of parental intuition is needed in assessing readiness for most milestones. And pediatricians who have studied and observed child development can guide us as well. In fact, the American Academy of Pediatrics (AAP) has set their standards for athletics and readiness.

As stated in the AAP parent website, Healthychildren.org: "As more and more children specialize in a single sport at a younger age, research suggests that they face a higher risk of overuse injuries from training, as well as an increase in potential for stress and burnout, according to a clinical report from the American Academy of Pediatrics-" (AAP, 2016)

Apart from figure skating, rhythmic gymnastics, and diving (where AAP acknowledges the need for further research on the long-term effects), the AAP recommends the following guidelines for preventing overuse injuries, stress, and burnout (AAP, 2016):

- Specialization (focusing on one sport) should be delayed until 15 to16 yrs. of age.
- Multiple sport play should be encouraged
- Prior to a child below the age of 15 specializing in a sport, a discussion with their pediatrician about their goals and "whether they are appropriate and realistic."
- Parents should monitor all training and coaching for elite programs
- A young athlete should take a hiatus from a sport for "at least three months during the year, in increments of one month" but continue to be physically active in other activities.
- One or two days per week should be sport free for young athletes (AAP, 2016).

Look at it this way: With 70% of our youths leaving sports by age of 13, before they hit high school (Miner, 2016), we have to ask why. By age 13, those that are competing at high levels are expected to specialize and the pressure to perform is significant. Elite teams and competitions induce a sense of pride and accomplishment for both parent and player, but don't be enticed by the glory without full knowledge of the inherent risks. Specializing too early can lead to a multitude of issues including potential physical and psychological harm.

Early specialization can also be isolating for a child. Specialization places travel demands and can mean loss of time at school. More and more, kids are being partially home-schooled to meet the travel requirements of their sport, leaving the athlete with inconsistent opportunity to be with friends in a purely social setting.

Additionally, the child often bears significant stress to perform given the financial and time commitments made by their parents. This stress can be a factor that causes the child to lose passion for a sport. The pressure creates a high potential for burnout, usually resulting in a child leaving the sport altogether.

Experts Weigh In On the Risks

Dr. Brenner, former chairperson of the AAP Council on Sports Medicine and Fitness, stated in his article titled "Sport Specialization and Intense Training in Young Athletes," published in the *Journal of Pediatrics*, "The ultimate goal of sports is for kids to have fun and learn lifelong physical activity skills. We want kids to have more time for deliberate play, where they can just go out and play with their friends and have fun-" (Brenner, 2016).

With 3 to 11% of all high school athletes going on to play at the college level and only 1% of all high school athletes getting college athletic scholarships, do the risks of specialization outweigh the rewards? And for those that have aspirations of a professional sports career, it should be noted that .03 to .5% of high school athletes ever make it to the pros (Brenner, 2016).

In the presence of this cautionary information, why specialize? Specialization has its place and can lead to higher success rates, as Dr. Brenner points out in his report, but the key, he states, is timing (Brenner, 2016). Based on research, early diversification in sports with specialization in late adolescence provides an athlete with the best recipe for success. Playing multiple sports early while delaying specializing allows the athlete a higher chance for optimal performance because they will reduce the risk of physical injury from overuse or burnout.

Dr. Brenner goes on to discuss the need for deliberate play in our youths over deliberate practice. Deliberate play is "the intentional and voluntary nature of informal sport games designed to maximize inherent enjoyment-" (Brenner, 2016). This is when a child plays a pickup game of basketball in the driveway with neighborhood kids or tosses a football with you in the backyard for example. Children that experience deliberate play in their early years statistically stay in sports longer and with greater success (Brenner, 2016). Encourage your athlete to go outside and have fun with sports.

Deliberate practice is a little different, in my opinion; it's any activity intentionally designed to increase performance with no immediate rewards. This is the training they do with their coaches or on their own time with specific drills aligned with specific goals such as a high-jumper practicing a certain head placement to gain more distance or a golfer practicing a specific hip rotation to execute more power in a given shot. This should be reserved for the late teen years.

To summarize, diversification and overall life balance are key for younger kids, which means taking breaks from an organized sport throughout the year. With the exception of some sports like gymnastics or diving, early specialization should be entered into only after serious consideration and discussion with your child's pediatrician. Delayed specialization will allow for the athlete to develop physically and emotionally so they're prepared to handle the rigors of specialization and able to excel in their sport of choice even under the additional pressure.

Understanding Your Child's Desires

After you have decided that your child is chronologically and physically ready to specialize, take the time to listen to your athlete. All too often parents come into my office claiming the child wants one thing. However, the child tells me something quite different when we have a one-on-one consultation. I try to remind parents to be active listeners in their child's life.

One of the easiest ways to train one's mind and brain to be in tune with your child is to practice empathy. I tell parents to spend a few minutes a day looking at life through their child's eyes. What does that child wake up to? Does the child run downstairs, greeted by a happy face or a barrage of dictations around what is expected of them that day? Is that child happy when you take them to practice or a game, or are they stressed that their performance might be met with ridicule?

You know your child better than anyone. This will not be a difficult task. The only difficulty will be for you to be honest with yourself. Remember, you don't have to share this task with anyone, and your findings are yours alone. But don't overlook what you uncover when you ask yourself these questions. Make necessary changes that will impact your athlete's mental game for the better. This could mean focusing on having fun, letting them set and achieve their own goals, or helping them adapt a growth mindset. Isn't the desired outcome for your athlete to have longevity in his or her sport? Because the longer an athlete plays a sport or sports, the more personal benefits they achieve throughout their lives.

In addition to seeing life through your child's eyes, you need to set up an environment that allows them to express their desires freely. They need to know that they can tell you anything without judgment and retribution if their desires for the future do not coincide with yours.

A father of a young baseball player told me that in addition to coaching his son's team, he spent a lot of time practicing together with his son. But he was quick to point out, "If he ever tells me, 'No, I don't want to throw the ball Dad,' then we don't do it. I never want him to feel this was forced on him, and that anything he gains from this sport is what he puts into it on his own." He went on to add that his son had worked for many years with a private coach. This coach was recruited by major league teams when he was in college, so he was very accomplished. And one day the son asked his private coach about his experiences with youth baseball. The coach was quick to point out that he played baseball, but he also played football and basketball. He encouraged the young man to play multiple sports, to learn and grow, both physically and mentally, so that when the player is older, he will have a wealth of multiple experiences in which to draw from. He went on to explain that he loved each sport for different reasons, but he played them for the fun—learning and personal growth were priceless byproducts of it.

In a CNBC interview, Anthony Robbins once said, "What controls your decisions are the patterns and habits you create in your life -" (Dill, 2017). If you create an environment that allows for open communication, your decisions and your athlete's decisions will be made based on an understanding of each other's desires and not on assumptions. Decisions based on assumptions can lead to family strife, angst, and regret for everyone. Give their psychological game a strong foundation and they will achieve their own excellence.

CHAPTER 8

Pressure

Watching your kids in sports can be a euphoric or nail-biting experience depending on the day. When they show up but their game doesn't, or when the game falls solely on their shoulders, you feel their stress and anxiety. However, no matter the sport, age, or level, an athlete facing difficulty has two choices: give up or push through. How many times have you watched an athlete endure difficulty and still finish well, if not on top, while another struggles and gives up emotionally? How many times have we asked ourselves, "How do I help them to perform under pressure?"

Dr. Nick

The evening of February 5, 2017, like most Americans, I was glued to my television, watching Super Bowl LI. By the end of the third quarter, the New England Patriots were 25 points behind the Atlanta Falcons. I assumed the score of 28-3 sealed the win for Atlanta. After all no team in Super Bowl history had ever overcome a double digit spread in the second half. I couldn't have been more wrong.

The New England Patriots, led by quarterback Tom Brady, turned the game around in the fourth quarter. With six minutes to go, the Patriots scored two touchdowns and two, two-point conversions to tie the game. In overtime, James White made the final winning touchdown, making the New England Patriots the first team to ever close a double digit spread going into the final quarter of a Super Bowl. The win can be attributed to New England's performance under pressure.

What Is Pressure?

There are typically two reactions to pressure in sports and life: succumbing to it and persevering in its presence.

Yet, some experts in the field of performance profess that pressure is not real, that pressure doesn't exist. They believe that pressure, such as time in a game, is simply there as a reality, another fact or component of playing a game. If this fact or component is ignored, and focus remains on the game itself, then pressure ceases to exist. For example, if there are three seconds left in a basketball game, the player has to shoot the basket the same way they would if there were 30 minutes left in the game—pressure can have no impact.

I do not subscribe to this theory. Pressure *does* exist and it does impact performance.

So, is there a universal definition of pressure? No. I guarantee that if I asked 100 individuals to define pressure, I would have 100 different answers. Pressure is about perception. Pressure is interpreted differently by each of us. What some think of as pressure, others wouldn't be phased by.

Under certain conditions, pressure can be felt by anyone. When the conscious mind interrupts the subconscious mind, pressure can manifest itself. Remember that the conscious mind is where learning and thinking take place. Once something is learned and embedded, it goes into the subconscious mind. Much of what we do daily, like driving a car, walking, or running, is performed by our subconscious—we don't have to think about it. The subconscious mind is our internal autopilot.

Athletes practice and train their muscles so they can perform basic skills without thinking about them. Trained basketball players don't think about how to shoot a ball as they're headed toward the basket. They dribble down the court and just take the shot. Most of an athlete's performance occurs in the subconscious. However, when pressure is introduced, we inflict thoughts that interrupt the subconscious automatic process and as a result, performance is hindered.

For example, a basketball player dribbles down the court and he sees he has two seconds to make the final winning shot. And let's suppose he thinks, *I've got to make this shot to win the game. Can I make this shot? The team will be mad if I don't make this.* At this point, the player's conscious mind has just interrupted the subconscious mind and created pressure. If you were that player, would you be able to make that shot?

A golfer hits almost every shot the same way—their swing is their swing—and it happens without thinking for most of the round. Yet, when the athlete is on the 18th tee box and just needs to par the last hole to win the tournament, there is potential for a conscious thought, such as worry or fear, to enter the mind. Once the player allows that thought in, his or her swing is no longer automatic. The subconscious mind is interrupted, and they are playing in the conscious mind, potentially altering their swing.

Let's think about this concept away from sports. A friend of mine broke her ankle. She explained, "I fell walking down my front steps. I literally missed the last step." Now, this person had lived in the same house for 17 years and had walked down those same steps every day. Why did she miss the step? Because as she told me, "I was worried about getting my son to his class, me to work, and we were running late. He was taking his time as usual and as I walked out the front door, my mind started to think, *There's going to be traffic now, and I'm going to be late for work!* And just like that, something she did every day became an issue because pressure became a factor.

Now does this mean we will always be met with failure or something negative when we worry and try to perform? No, of course not. But when we add pressure, the opportunity to interrupt the mind enough to go off course is present.

Have you ever had that day when it seems as if you can do nothing right, when even the most basic tasks are met with failure? And did that day start out with bad news or something inducing stress into your day? I would expect that both questions would be met with a yes answer. Most of us have had many days like that. If we analyze those days, I surmise most of us could find a root cause of the stress that derailed us from the tasks we do on autopilot every day.

Conversely, have you ever had those days when everything works like clockwork? Of course you have. You wake up on time, you like what you're wearing, you feel good, and you're relaxed. You're running on full autopilot and things seem to just flow. That's because you have no stress, no pressure is interrupting your subconscious, and you're performing at your highest level.

Why Do Our Thoughts Interrupt Our Flow?

Time is one typical source of pressure in sports. The clock of any game can induce pressure because of the need for the athlete to get the job done within a certain amount of time. Imagine you're at the basket with three seconds on the clock and you take the shot. Will that shot be performed exactly the same as if you'd had 30 minutes left in the game? The answer depends on the athlete, but for some, a game clock can create pressure, which could alter performance.

In sports, some pressures such as time are induced by the game. But some other pressures such as coaches, teammates, and internal goals are induced by the player. I consider these to be self-induced pressures. Knowing what the pressures are will not change the fact that they are there. The only variable that can be altered is the athlete. The athlete must train to handle pressures to maintain good performance.

Do you feel any less guilty for something that is rational than you do for something that is irrational? No, of course not. Guilt is guilt, no matter the cause. The same goes for pressure. Pressure is pressure, but its roots vary by individual. Yet, a parent or coach can identify some triggers before competition if we examine the realities of the athlete's sport and we understand the parameters of the game. For example, in golf, potential triggers could be course condition, weather, or course length. In each sport, the potential stress points must be addressed before competition, and must be included in how we train the athlete. As we discussed previously, deep, dedicated practices should include pressure to effectively prepare the athlete for competition.

When there's pressure on an individual, there are two possible outcomes: they thrive, or they succumb. The athlete who thrives is seemingly motivated by pressure or their focus is increased by it. The pressure actually moves him or her to a hyper-focused state. These athletes immediately focus on what needs to get done. Tiger Woods, for one, is famous for producing amazing results under pressure. Clearly, Tom Brady demonstrated this same quality in leading his team to that Super Bowl LI comeback win.

On the other hand, the athlete who crumbles under pressure does so because they have conscious thoughts that interrupt the subconscious and so their focus is diminished or lost. Australian pro golfer Jason Day, on the third day of the 2017 PGA Championship, was on the 18th tee and four strokes from the lead (Sobel, 2017). He hit his tee shot into trees. Most golfers would play this safe, but Jason went for a hook shot. He claims he's done this shot many times without fail. Yet on that day, he did fail and landed the shot in a row of bushes where he had to take a drop. The next shot got him out of the bushes but into the thick rough, where he took another shot, landing short of the green. A few more shots, and the ball made it to the hole for a staggering quadruple-bogey. Not bad for a weekend hacker, but for one of the world's best players, it was horrifying.

After that round, Day walked off without speaking to the press but is quoted as saying just before the opening round that week, "…I'm like, 'My game is not where it should be. I'm not doing the right things on the course. I really haven't had the greatest year.' You're not panicking or anything. You're just wondering why. You're up at night thinking about, 'Ok what do I need to do to get back to winning form?' I think once I minimize the distractions in my life and can focus more on playing golf and focus, and single-focus on golf, then everything will take care of itself-" (Sobel, 2017).

The distractions or pressures Day referred to, included his mother's lung cancer diagnosis—an enormous worry that could put anyone's performance in question. But not all pressures have the same impact on everyone. Remember: pressure is perception. No matter what the pressures are, their presence in the player's mind can significantly alter their performance.

Why do athletes differ in their reactions to pressure? The answer is simple. An athlete's reaction to pressure is directly linked to temperament, grit, and self-efficacy. The more grit and self-efficacy possessed by the athlete, the better their performance under pressure. In the case of Jason Day, he was able to be so close to the top on that third day, prior to the 18th hole, even with such family strife. That speaks volumes to his levels of grit and self-efficacy.

Individuals with high levels of grit and self-efficacy possess passion, perseverance, a low need for positive reinforcement, and knowledge they can get the job done in high-pressure situations. These athletes know they possess the skill set to accomplish whatever is necessary. Think again of the example of the athlete who has three seconds left in the game and needs to make the shot to win the game for the team. The player who knows he can do it will not consciously question, "Can I do this?" The lack of self-questioning allows the player to remain focused and allows all their training to get the job done.

Low or nonexistent levels of grit and self-efficacy equate to higher levels of self-doubt. There is an inverse relationship between grit/self-efficacy and sensitivity/doubt. The higher the grit/self-efficacy levels, the lower the sensitivity/doubt levels, and vice versa. Same example as before—three seconds left in the game—does the player make the shot if he or she has low levels of grit and self-efficacy? Probably not, and if they do make it, it's luck. When that player takes the shot, their skills are running on interrupted autopilot and they are not executing effectively.

How Do We Stop Pressure From Impacting Performance?

We never know what an athlete is capable of until competition. Times of stress are the best opportunities to demonstrate abilities. The main reasons my clients initially seek my help are issues with performance under pressure. Their skill sets are at a high level, but they fall short of their goals because they succumb to pressure. Before we talk strategies, the first step in my treatment is to administer a TAIS test.

A TAIS test, Test of Attentional and Interpersonal Style, measures overall one's levels of focus and how sensitive one is to distractions. This same test is utilized in business, sports, and the military. It measures qualities such as awareness, internal and external distractibility, confidence, and sensitivity to criticism. Each of my clients takes this test so I have a baseline from which to work in getting them to focus under pressure. Yet, with all these years of testing athletes, I can say the highly sensitive, easily distracted athlete will fall to pressure at rapid speed compared to those with low sensitivity and high focus levels.

Training is the solution to pressure. I once read a quote by a Navy Seal about performing under pressure, "…you don't rise to the occasion, you sink to the level of your training…-" (Schrage, 2015). These words relate to any athlete under pressure. The Navy SEALs train for 75% of their time and deploy for 25% of their time because they understand that training is the key to execution under high-pressure conditions (Barker, 2015). The higher the performance levels, the greater the training. Navy SEALs have the highest level of training in the armed forces because they are an elite fighting division. Their missions demand precision.

Imagine the SEALs that went in to take down Osama Bin Laden, the world's most wanted terrorist. I don't think anyone can imagine that level of pressure. Yet they completed their mission successfully because they trained for it. Not the day before or for a few hours a week. They trained day and night over a long period of time. They trained for it like a prima ballerina trains and memorizes a routine, so she can perform without a misstep.

Like Anthony Robbins (1991) said, "Repetition is the mother of skill." Training and repetition go hand in hand to embed a skill into our subconscious. The more training, the deeper the embedding, and ultimately the higher the performance. The higher the grit and self-efficacy, the lower the sensitivity to pressure, whether external or internal.

Training Is Not the Same as Learning

Now there is a difference between learning and training. Training doesn't require understanding. Training requires you to do as instructed over and over until the skill is mastered. You don't always know why you do it, but you do it.

Think back to when you were taught multiplication tables. Most of us who are now adults had to memorize them when we were kids. Did you learn them? Meaning, did you understand the logic behind them? No, at the age of 8, very few, if any of us, understood the logic behind them. Yet we knew that 2x2 equaled 4. Why? Because we were trained. We were, in fact, trained so hard that the skill became embedded to a point that we never forgot our times tables.

So, with your athlete, train, train, and train to reduce the effect of pressure on their performance. But I caution you: before you have your six-year-old in the driveway shooting a hundred baskets a day, re-read our chapters on setting goals, practice, and assessing readiness. Keep the training age- and skill-appropriate. Incorporate goals and make sure your athlete is the one setting and achieving them on their own.

Despite solid training, it is possible for an athlete to have a thought that seeps into their conscious. I instruct them to focus on one task during competition and let the subconscious handle the rest. This allows his or her training, embedded in their subconscious, to perform the necessary physical movements.

Let's revisit the example of my high-jumper client. She knew she could perform the jump that she wanted. Yet, her mind blocked her performance because her thoughts always drifted to fears of failing. When I instructed her to think of one specific part of the execution of that jump, such as her head placement, it occupied her mind so worry could not interrupt her subconscious. After that, she performed the jump without a problem.

Go back to the chapter on practice and review the techniques on imagery. All of those techniques are highly effective in reducing pressure's effects of performance.

Why Competition Is Important

I have a client who worked at a youth camp for golf. The director that ran the camp told him specifically that there were to be no competitive games. He just wanted the campers to be taught how to swing the clubs. This camp was four hours long, for kids ages 6 to 10. My client said, "This is incredibly difficult because the little kids are begging to play a game. They naturally want a competitive situation to make it fun." My young client obliged the youths out of empathy, and he was reprimanded for it. When he questioned the director, the director said, "I don't want hurt feelings because someone didn't win."

Protecting kids from failure, and not consciously finding situations where they can develop higher levels of grit sets them up for failure in the future. Isn't it better for a five-year-old to learn they can lose than to end up with a college-aged kid who has to accept failure for the first time? There is a reason why competition exists early in life. Removing outs from baseball, implementing a "there are no winners" rule, or giving everyone a trophy at the end of the season is not innocuous. It is extremely harmful and preventative to a human's development of mental strength.

I shake my head at situations like this. Hurt feelings are part and parcel of failure. Remember that the biggest internal motivator is wanting to avoid pain. Knowing the pain associated with failure, an individual will work harder to avoid failing in the future. Therefore, if approached appropriately, failure is an opportunity to grow and develop. Athletes become better players because they've failed; they become mentally stronger because they've failed. Do not protect your youth from this growth opportunity. Better they learn it early on than later in life. Later in life is when true pressure shows up. Being a good parent or coach entails preparing kids to handle pressure. And, there is no better place to get training for handling pressure than sports.

Not all competition is created equal and that's why I think sports are an integral part of a child's exposure to pressure situations. Because competition in sports is the only true way to measure performance. It's the only time each individual is measured on the exact same parameters. You don't have that same outcome in education or work, for example. Schools vary, teachers vary, tests vary so that an A in Mrs. X's class can be very different from an A in Mr. Y's class, even if they are teaching the exact same material.

So, given this fact, sports are an amazing way to see development in our youths and to foster life skills that transcend the athletic world. Through sports, kids learn that hard work fosters grit, self-efficacy, the importance of a growth mindset, and how to handle pressure. But none of these lessons are possible without competition. So, I ask: Why do we then remove competition from sports for our younger athletes?

Recently, I asked a college coach about the one thing his players lack when they arrive freshman year. He said, "I'd say confidence but that's not it. I think it's that they can't handle expectations. They aren't prepared for the demands of schoolwork and training for the team. Some just weren't ready for not being the number one player anymore, as they were on their high school team, and while some team members are competing, they have to stay back to train, train, and train."

This coach went on to say, "I coach a Division III school and by the time they get to me, they are deflated because they didn't make Division I. This dream had been preached to them since they started. So, I have to use freshman year to build them up to where they can handle the pressures of collegiate sports. I have to get them to realize that they can compete on the same level as Division I players, but they have to put in the work to get there."

As I continued my conversation with the college coach, he told me a story about a player with whom he had a disagreement about his performance. His parents had taken to Twitter to take jabs at the coach in defense of their son. Over time, when cooler heads prevailed and they saw positive changes in their son, the parents finally realized what the coach was trying to do—instill grit and self-efficacy. Eventually, the parents approached the coach to apologize and said, "What you did with him, we could never do." This coach told me, "If parents stop running to their kid's defense, and stop doing seemingly small things for these kids, they will develop the skills necessary to persevere in life."

Social Pressure and Coach Pressure

As I have stated earlier, pressure either exists due to parameters of the sport, such as time, or its self-induced. Any pressure an athlete feels that enters their minds and interrupts their performance, is real. Athletes will even drop out of a sport over these social pressures. When a client tells me that they feel pressure from a coach or peers, they don't understand why I term that being self-induced. They ask, "Why is it my doing if someone else is doing it to me?"

Pressure is perception, as I stated in the beginning. I ask my patients, "Are you giving more attention to what people are saying or what you need to do? If you, the athlete, gives attention to something, then you hold responsibility for it." This is self-induced pressure. And again, I instruct the athlete to use the imagery techniques, previously described to regain focus.

The athletes that struggle with social pressure are typically those with a predisposition to lower thresholds of grit and self-efficacy. Once we can enhance the athlete's levels on those attributes, combined with the self-regulation techniques (imagery), the athlete can perform without disruption.

Once, I was working with a young client before he went off to compete in a US Amateur event. We were working on the putting green, and he hit one putt beautifully. Of course, he made it. Now, I stopped him and asked, "Did you see the ladybug?"

He answered, "What ladybug?"

"The one right there. Your ball went right past it. It was in your line."

Then he saw the ladybug and said, "Oh, no I didn't."

"If that were me putting," I told him, "I would have had to move the bug. It would have distracted me."

That moment exemplifies the kind of focus an athlete needs to perform at a high level. This athlete's sole focus was on the ball going into the hole. He wasn't noticing other potential distractions, things that would have caused someone like myself to lose focus. He knew he could make the putt, and he allowed his subconscious to do the stroke it needed to do without bringing in negative thoughts to interrupt his flow.

Understand that this is easier for some individuals than it is for others. Pressure is perception, and each player perceives different things as pressure for different reasons. If, as a coach and/or parent, you can develop their grit, self-efficacy, and ability to focus in competition, then some of those distractions will decrease, if not cease altogether. Now, sometimes new pressures are introduced in life, but once these skill sets are learned, then the player will automatically know how to handle the new stressors.

CHAPTER 9

Hidden Dangers

In a world where homogenization is revered, and difference can spark disdain and ridicule, we must stop and assess. Why do we, as parents, educators, coaches, and mentors feel the need to push our youths toward the norm: the well-traveled path? Is it fear—fear of the unknown, fear of failure, fear of missing out, or fear of recrimination? A healthy dose of fear keeps us in check, and some amount is vital for survival, but when we impose our fears in the form of demands on our kids, we fail them. Following the pack or keeping up with the Joneses is never the correct answer, but many of us are guilty of it.

Our kids get on this treadmill of sports because of parents, coaches, or teammates. There isn't a minute of free time anymore for them to just be kids. I can't remember the last time I saw kids playing a game outside until dinner time. They just don't have the time for it anymore. We've scheduled every free minute of our kid's lives so they don't get behind the pack, so they have an edge. But what is the cost? Everything has a price.

Raising children is like walking through a minefield sometimes. And though our ultimate goal is to raise good kids, successful kids who will become happy adults, there are many pitfalls along the way. Navigating sports is no different. When my child was competing in junior golf tournaments, I worried about many things such as labels others placed on him and how that affected how he viewed himself. Was he just following the pack, caught up in the rush instead of following his own passion? And was he burning out?

No matter how many times I told him, "Golf is something you do, it's not who you are," I'm not sure it was understood. Holding impressive labels can give an athlete a sense of strength and belief in themselves and can empower them to keep performing at high levels. Success begets more success, right? But can it ever be too much? If your athlete is a consistently high performer, can the labels that others and even you—knowingly or unknowingly—place on them be harmful? Can following the pack be the best thing for your athlete? And can you identify a child who is burned-out and what the next steps are to help?

Dr. Nick

We navigate many minefields in our daily lives. Young athletes face trials and tribulations every day in school, sports, with friends, and even with family. In sports specifically, labeling, following the pack, and burn out are some of the biggest and most challenging issues for athletes.

Labels

Society is full of labels. Labeling is how we categorize each other. Most times, we are completely unaware we are labeling. And we don't always understand the expectations that are associated with these labels. It's common for parents to purchase baseball mitts or buy toy trucks when they learn they are having a boy, for example. There's an expectation that their boy will fall in step with male stereotypes. Does that always happen? No, but the expectations parents have for their children are there, and failure to meet those expectations can be emotionally damaging for both a parent and a child.

Labeling our athletes, such as "gifted" or "prodigy," can mean riddling them with unspoken expectations. These labels, despite a parent believing they are being supportive, can backfire and cause poor performance. For example, a former patient of mine told his mother that he could identify a tough competitor on the first tee: "If the kid walked up and introduced themselves and said little else other than normal pleasantries, I knew he could play well. But when I met them on the tee box and either they, their parents, or both went on and on about the recent tournaments they played and how well they did, I knew the kid wasn't that good. There was never a time in all my years of competing that this theory proved untrue."

Why did that young man's theory never prove untrue? Because, if you have to sell it then it's not there to begin with—it's not organic. One's performance should speak to one's ability. Their mouths or the mouths of their parents don't need to. When clients come into my office and the parent is talking the child up, I become acutely aware that this propaganda may be negatively impacting their child's performance. Parents don't bring their athletes to me if they are excelling in their performance. They come to me when their mental game isn't matching their physical abilities. Often, the athlete's head is cluttered with expectations derived from the parents. Again, labels translate into expectations that can burden them and impact their performance.

As we discussed in earlier chapters, if the athlete is consumed with worries such as self-doubt, fear of disappointing others, or pressure to perform at a specific level, then their focus is not on the performance itself. If the athlete is trying to live up to a label or overcome a label on the playing field, that is where their mind will be and not on the game. That can manifest into poor performance.

I know a golf pro that has stated, "If I had a dime for every time a parent came to me wanting lessons for their child and ended the conversation with, 'They are a super athlete,' or an 'amazing athlete,' I'd be a wealthy man. In my experience, no young child is amazing at anything other than sleeping and eating." Now, many parents reading this may be up in arms with the golf pro's comments, but there is some truth in his statements.

What are the expectations we communicate as parents or as coaches when we use certain labels? And how do those expectations impact the athlete? It's easy for parents to dole out the exaggerated labels of prodigy, star, or gifted when describing their athletes, but what is the cost?

Expectations can breed insecurities, whether the expectations are too high or too low. If young people are told they can't do something or that they aren't good enough, they tend to believe it, and it becomes a self-fulfilling prophecy. Conversely, if all a child hears is that they are a prodigy, a star, or a gifted athlete, they too, bear a heavy burden. The expectation could be interpreted by the athlete as enormous pressure to always perform, and if they fail, they will fall short of their coach's or their parent's thoughts of them.

When parents profess that a child is a gifted athlete, are they correct? The definitions of gifted vary amongst different organizations. However, the National Association for Gifted Children says: "Gifted individuals are those who demonstrate outstanding levels of aptitude (defined as an exceptional ability to reason and learn) or competence (documented performance or achievement in top 10% or rarer) in one or more domains-" (NAGC, 2010). Given this definition, mislabeling is easy in a parent's eyes. We see our children for all the good they do, but not all parents see their children's imperfections.

The definition of prodigy is more definitive however, stating that prodigies are usually "children who demonstrate professional abilities before the age of 10-" (Roos, 2014). Prodigies are quite rare, and we do not see them often in society. Therefore, use of this label must be done with great caution. Putting an athlete in the prodigy bracket can create an overly embellished sense of self or an expectation that is far too intense for a young athlete.

I anticipate that many of you reading this are throwing up your hands saying, "I can't say anything too negative to my athlete or too positive, so what do I say?" It's a valid question and the answer is simple. In fact, I go back to what I have said in previous chapters. When giving praise or criticism, keep your comments specific and growth minded. Specific to performance could mean saying something such as, "I liked the way you stepped into your swing today. You made good contact with the ball." Or, "The way you anticipated your opponent's next move on the court today was on point, and you were able to return the ball effectively." Keep the praise specific, providing useful information the athlete can use during future competitions. Use growth-minded words and focus on what they learned, not if they won or lost.

When you keep your comments specific and use growth-minded talk, make sure you follow up with questions. Ask your athlete what they learned from how they played that day. Make learning of prime importance for any athletic event, reinforcing that win or lose, something can be gained by the player. Parents should guide but not dictate, support but not take over. Asking your player questions puts them in the driver seat.

In *Mindset*, Carol Dweck sums up the effects of labels on both fixed and growth mindsets. She says:

"…in the fixed mindset, both positive and negative labels can mess with your mind. When you're given a positive label, you're afraid of losing it, and when you're hit with a negative label, you're afraid of deserving it-" (Dweck, 2006).

"When people are in a growth mindset, stereotypes don't disrupt their performance. The growth mindset takes the teeth out of the stereotype and makes people better able to fight back. They don't believe in permanent inferiority. And if they are behind, well, then they'll work harder and try to catch up-" (Dweck, 2006).

Knowing your mindset and your athlete's mindset is imperative to understanding how labels have impacted the athlete. The goal should be to make the athlete more growth minded, making the athlete better equipped to handle imposed labels from others. I say others, because as parents and coaches you can only control what *you* do; you can't control what others do. Arming your athlete with the right mental attributes and adjusting your behavior will allow them to handle the labels imposed by others.

Following the Pack

Vince Papale and Jim Morris are examples of athletes that took the less traveled road toward playing in the pros. Both had their stories immortalized on the big screen for the world to see in the movies "Invincible" and "The Rookie", respectively. Vince, a multisport athlete in high school, tried out for the Philadelphia Bell of the World Football League and became a wide receiver. After his success with that team he was drafted by the Eagles, making him the oldest rookie in the NFL at the age of 30 (Quackenbush, 2009). Jim Morris was a high school baseball coach, who went on to play professionally after he made a bet with his players. He told them that if they won the district championship, he would try out. He got on the Tampa Bay Devils in 2000 and played for two seasons before injuries brought his major league career to an end (Richard Moss, 2018). Neither of these two individuals took the conventional route to the pros, but both made it there because they possessed growth mindset, grit, and self-efficacy. They understood the importance of goal setting and a strong practice routine.

Today, the introduction of many elite teams for all sports has created a definite class system in youth sports. Most college recruiters don't care if you played a sport in high school. They are more interested in what elite teams you have played on. Football is only played in high school, so it is the exception to that rule. This atmosphere generates the idea that if you aren't good enough to play travel or elite, then you are done playing that sport. Playing for fun, exercise, and social development no longer exists.

For all the talk of mindset and grit, the actual application is minimal. I hear parents talk about how their son or daughter needs to get on the "A team" or else their sports lives will be over. I've heard multiple stories of parents complaining that their child wasn't picked for a team because of unfair practices. Given that parents are usually the ones running these travel teams, I believe some amount of favoritism is at play and that true skill assessment can be falling in the hands of unqualified assessors. Yet parents have to ask, at such young ages, does it really matter? Isn't this time in an athlete's life about learning and developing as a player? Is it really that critical to be on the "A team?"

On the flip side, I applaud those who see the benefits of the "B" or "C" teams. Remember, it's not about the team your 11-year-old makes, but the amount of playing time they get on a team. If your player will flourish on a "B" or "C" team because they will have more time to hone their skills and develop that all-important self-efficacy around their abilities, shouldn't that be the goal?

The goal most definitely shouldn't be about what others see. Playing a sport isn't about fostering the parental social agenda and keeping up with the Joneses. Ask yourself, "Am I upset that Jonny didn't get on the 'A team' for him, or am I worried about what others think or will say?"

One of the toughest jobs we do is being a parent, especially being an effective one for our children. Even the most well-meaning, loving parent makes mistakes. That is why this chapter is so important. It may be toward the end of the book, but it is crucial for anyone with a young athlete in their life. Parents have to accept things they may not like, that don't follow the norm, or don't coincide with plans they had for their children's future. How we handle those moments are crucial to the emotional well-being of a child.

A friend of mine has two sons who are solid baseball players in a competitive town for baseball. During the off season, she found out accidentally that their travel team teammates, who are friends, joined an indoor training club and didn't tell them. Now this mother, who definitely focuses on what's best for her boys, felt a bit slighted, but ultimately, she felt her kids needed this time away from the sport. I agreed.

Note, a cutthroat, backstabbing environment does exist in youth sports and getting caught up in it doesn't help your athlete. This woman's sons made their high school team and are doing exceptionally well, even better than some who attended that training in the off-season. More is not always better. And too much of a good thing can backfire.

Inevitably, when parents ask me things like, "I heard about this club team or tournament that so and so is doing. Should 'we' be signing up too? Will 'we' be left behind?" First, I caution any and all parents against using the pronoun "we". Be careful. The person who is doing the performing is your athlete, and they are the ones who should be driving the bus of what they do and don't do with your guidance.

That means that the drive and push to do more in the way of practice, games, or tournaments should solely come from the athlete. You can certainly enlighten them to the opportunities, and you can exemplify a growth mindset, self-efficacy, and grit on a consistent basis, but the ownership of the athlete's goals should come from the athlete.

Second, I caution parents from following what the kids next door are doing—the proverbial "keeping up with the Joneses." What everyone else is doing may or may not be what's best for your athlete, and to you that's all that should matter. Use what they are doing as an idea to present, mull over, and contemplate, but don't make it a pressure point to get on their treadmill. Following what another family chooses to sign their athlete up for or compete in can be a recipe for unnecessary pressure and angst for your athlete.

Identifying Burnout

Both Vince Papale and Jim Morris sought different career paths before they went back to their true passion. Sometimes in life you need to walk away from something before you can see how important the dream is to you. Your athlete may or may not have that moment when they want to quit or change, but you have to be ready to guide and accept their desires. In the end, this is about them, not about the parents or coaches, scholarships or the pros.

The staggering statistic that 70% of our youths leave organized sports by the age of 13 (Miner, 2016), should give everyone pause. We need to ask ourselves two questions: Why are they leaving? And what are the negative effects of them leaving? They leave because the sport is no longer fun for them. And when they leave, they miss out on developing key life skills like teamwork, time management, and physical activity. That's all before we discuss the embedding of attributes discussed in our earlier chapters like grit, self-efficacy, and goal setting. The ramifications for kids quitting sports too early are numerous and harmful for their overall development.

Over multiple decades, there has been a shift in how children engage in organized sporting activities. Youths used to begin organized sports later in life; most played pickup games in their neighborhoods and parks with friends and neighbors. By the middle grades, most youths played for their recreation departments and moved on to their high school teams.

In today's society, children begin organized sports in their toddler years. Parents sign their little ones up as soon as they are ready for preschool and some even before that. If a child shows aptitude in anything, the parental radar kicks in. Elite teams and private coaching are sought out for our athletes at an earlier and earlier age. Schools and recreation department sports are being pushed aside at an alarming rate to elite and private team play. We are privatizing youth sports.

Parents are spending significant sums of money to train and promote their young players. This push places many families in the path of financial peril and many athletes in the path of early burnout. Well-meaning parents get caught up in the hype of good marketing and hopes for college athletics, and they fail to see that specialization breeds an environment of increased pressure and decreased fun. Do not discount fun, since for passion to develop, there must be some interpretation of fun.

Many of my clients' parents spend thousands of dollars every year to keep their athlete in equipment, coaches, teams, and travel costs. The costs are even higher for those that decide a private education will also enhance their athlete's marketability.

What all these elite teams and private coaches fail to relay to the money-dishing parents is that only 1% of high school athletes get a college athletic scholarship and that only 3% to 11% of high school athletes play a sport in college (Brenner, 2016). Is the push and financial strain worth it if the risk is so high for the child to leave the sport and so low for them to play in college? You do the math.

The benefits of this change: athletes develop greater skill sets earlier on through more intense practice and play time. But is that really what is best for a 10- to 13-year-old child? As we discussed previously, the American Academy of Pediatrics is a huge supporter of deferring specialization and promoting multiple sports activities—not only to reduce the increase of physical injuries and overuse of muscles but also to promote emotional health. Emotionally, specialization puts the athlete at greater risk for burn-out because playing stops being fun for the athlete when it's too structured (AAP, 2016).

Yes, society structured fun right out the door, and burn out walked right in.

A parent of a young client once asked me, "How do I know if my child is burnt out or they just don't want to play anymore? And what do I do about it?" This is a very valid question and one I get frequently. How I mark burn-out in the athletes I see is when the athlete reports they are no longer having fun. There is almost a depressed quality to their explanation of how it's no longer fun. If they aren't claiming a lack of fun but want to stop and play something or try something else, then it's simply a change.

Either way, parents have to stop and listen to what their athlete is telling them in their words and actions. If the athlete no longer shows concern, dedication, or motivation toward playing, then certainly a discussion is necessary. Take the time to let your athlete tell you what they are feeling. In order for their feelings to flow freely, you have to let them know it's okay—and that you will support them no matter what.

Do you remember the father I discussed in the chapter on grit who I called Greg? His boys both ended up playing college football. Greg was all too aware that his boys were good players, but freely acknowledged they were never going any further with the sport beyond college. He had open conversations with them about this and made it clear that they should play because they loved it. He didn't want them to continue playing in college to please him or anyone else. He told me that he would do a check-in every once in a while. Greg would ask this one simple question, "Are you still having fun?" Why would he ask that question? In his words, "I wanted to give them an out. To let them know I supported them either way."

For intense parents who've had their hearts set on their child playing their sport in college and beyond, an athlete leaving a sport can be a tough change to absorb and get behind. In my experience, typically, the parents blame themselves. They believe they have failed the athlete and immediately try to make changes to induce fun for the child. Sometimes it works for a while, but often it doesn't. Again, parents need to listen to what the child is telling them and make it okay for the athlete to walk away from a sport.

Parents need to abandon the theory that if you quit at something then you will be a quitter for life. It simply is not true. There is no evidence to support that if an athlete quits playing a sport that they'll quit at everything else in life. Accepting that an athlete has either outgrown something or is experiencing burnout may be disheartening, but for their emotional well-being, parents need to guide and support them.

Once it's determined a child wants to leave a sport they have played with intensity for many years, leaving may not be simple. Frequently, the player's identity is tied to the sport they play—it's who they see themselves as. Once that identity is removed, they may feel less pressure on one hand, but feel completely lost on another.

I had a client who chose to leave competitive junior golf after competing for many years. He had experienced much success in golf, and it's how he and everyone else identified him. The loss of pressure was welcomed, but his parents came to me and asked why he seemed to be lost, almost not sure which way to turn.

This is the point when we need to allow the child to mourn the loss of this identity. It's something they have coveted for years and now it's gone. Time, understanding, and refocusing is necessary for healing. Now, in the case of my client, he eventually poured himself into another passion and prospered.

Again, this is where I want parents and coaches to understand that athletes should not get so wrapped up in a sport that their whole identity is attached to it. The sport is what they do, not who they are. Emotional health relies on a positive view of oneself. No young player should see themselves merely as a sports player. They should see themselves for their many intrinsic attributes. If their identity is wrapped up in the sport, then they are only as good as their last game or competition. That can cause the sport to no longer be fun and induce burn-out. It's a vicious cycle that you and your player should avoid because it's hard to get off of.

Now, understand the burned-out player or "need for a change player" is different from the "throwing a fit" player who storms off the field vowing to quit after a bad game. Burn-out or changing a sport requires conversation and finding the root cause. It will take time to come to this decision, and often the player will have put a lot of thought into it before you approach him or her.

I had a client who was a shoo-in for playing Division III Tennis. A bright child, he applied for many top schools but was not accepted to most of them because the competition was that high. His parents were more than disappointed. However, the school he got into and eventually went to didn't have tennis as a sport, just as a club. He joined the club and ended up playing the best tennis of his life. Why? Because it became about fun again and he was able to focus on the game, enhancing his performance. Sometimes taking a step back can help us go forward. Allow your athlete to take a break if they need it. It's okay.

CHAPTER 10

Extreme Parenting

Imagine you are on the sidelines watching your child up at bat and beaming at how excited he is to be playing baseball. A parent stands beside you and starts a conversation, "Is that your kid?"

"Yes."

"He's pretty good. What summer teams do you have him on?"

You, "Well, none."

The parent backs up, aghast, "Really?"

"Why?"

"He's a good player. I would have thought you'd have him on a club or summer travel team at least."

"Is your son playing this summer?"

"Oh yes. We spend all summer running from field to field. He's on multiple teams and sometimes he's asked to play up if the older kids are low on players. It's competitive out there, and the more playing the better. You want him to play in high school and college, right?"

"He's seven. I just want him to have fun. I haven't thought about high school, let alone college."

The other parent is speechless, looking at you like you committed a mortal sin and moves to another group of parents.

You give a wave to your little slugger who made it to first base, and you wonder to yourself, *Am I being neglectful or is this other parent going way overboard?*

Dr. Nick

Parenting is the most difficult job anyone will ever have and like anything else, some people are better at it than others. Even the best parents have had times where they didn't make appropriate or good parenting decisions. Perhaps they used words that were too harsh, or they didn't provide the best guidance for their child's age, for example. Nothing or no one is 100%, a 100% of the time. To err is human, as they say.

We previously discussed several parenting styles: authoritative, authoritarian, permissive, and neglectful. In chapter 1, we noted every parent fits into one style overall and to varying degrees. However, there are parents whose authoritarian parenting style is so intense they have created a separate parenting category I have labeled as "extreme parenting." Extreme parenting is detrimental to a child; in fact, it's just as damaging as the permissive—parent with no rules—and the neglectful parenting style—the one who is not involved at all.

Nowhere is extreme parenting on full display more than in youth sports, where coveted college scholarships and dreams of going pro loom. Whether at an individual or team sporting event, some of these extreme parents stick out like a beacon in the night. Others are much more subtle in their extreme parenting, but both are just as damaging to the child.

What Is Helicopter Parenting vs. Steamroller Parenting?

There are two categories of extreme parents: helicopter and steamroller. Like the popular label suggests, a helicopter parent is one who metaphorically hovers over their child to an inappropriate level. A common definition is: "A person who is overly involved in their children's life-" (Merriam-Webster, n.d.). Helicopter parents typically involve themselves in every aspect of the child's life down to every detail, which may include choosing friends, organizing their free time, preparing their homework, pushing the schools so they get specific academic teachers, and monitoring their grades to an excess. A helicopter parent's main objective is to ensure their child has the perfect experience in sports, academia, and their social life. They strive to protect the child from any negativity or failure.

In sports, helicopter parents are the ones always aware of what other parents are doing for their kids. These parents will do anything to make sure their athlete doesn't miss a step and is even one step ahead of the pack. These parents are always hovering to ensure their player is handled fairly by coaches and other players. Obtaining the perfect experience from athletics for their player is the ultimate goal of the helicopter parent.

Steamroller parents, as I call them, or as I've also seen them referred to as "snow plough" parents, are just as controlling as helicopter parents, but their motivation is different. They're less motivated by a perfect experience than results—the perfect or most successful outcome is what these parents are after. These parents dictate instead of guide, demand instead of teach, and control instead of empower their athletes. Not unlike helicopter parents, they control every aspect of the child's life, predetermining what's best for their child's future and then taking the child along for the ride.

In sports, steamroller parents are often on the sidelines, yelling instructions, talking to the coach; they're all over their kid, perhaps recording their performance or taking pictures to an excess. And it appears their sole purpose is to control any and all outcomes for their child "for the sake of their future." They steamroll over everyone, including their child, to get results.

It's important to note that both of these extreme parenting types are about controlling every situation to guarantee an outcome. Extreme parents rarely address the child's desires or wants. Many extreme parents proclaim they know either what the child wants or that they know what's best for their child's future. What differentiates the two styles, again, is motive.

Before you start denouncing the existence of extreme parents or labeling yourself as a helicopter or steamroller parent, keep the following in mind: the amount of control you exert over your child's life and the consistency to which you apply that control.

For example: if your five-year-old wants to walk to school by himself and you say no, that alone does not make you a hovering or controlling parent. It's not excessive or inappropriate to walk a five-year-old to and from school—it is, in fact, good parenting. However, if you are walking your high schooler to and from school, keeping up with their friends on social media, monitoring their grades online throughout the day, making sure they are signed up for all the elite teams, deciding what colleges they should target, what the best major for them will be, or hiring someone to write their college essay for them, then you might want to ask yourself the question: *Am I an extreme parent?* In other words: *Do I hover or control far beyond what is reasonable for my child's age?*

Whenever I advise college coaches on prospective recruits, the most frequently asked question is: "What are the parents like?" In fact, the parent-child dynamic is a critical part of a college coach's decision to recruit or not recruit. No matter how good the player, if the coach thinks they will be dealing with difficult, meddling parents, it will significantly impact their decision in a negative way.

Golf Digest published an article about an LPGA player and her coach, I have chosen not to name, who had severed their ties with each other (Diaz, 2016). In the article, her former coach claimed the player's parents were the quintessential helicopter parents and that their parenting style negatively impacted his ability to effectively coach. He went on to detail how this young woman's father controlled her every move in life, such as when she slept, when she practiced, and even worse, every detail of how she practiced.

The renowned coach recounted a time when the player's father hovered over her before a tournament. The father reportedly dished out a barrage of instructions, instead of allowing for the space and quiet any professional golfer needs before a critical round. The intense instruction from the father created doubt in the player's mind. Not surprisingly, she didn't bring home the desired win she was clearly capable of (Diaz, 2016).

The LPGA player's coach was not the only one who has walked away from a job they loved because of overbearing parents. A high school basketball coach in Michigan, Clayton Castor, walked off the job at the end of his most successful season where he'd been named ABC Coach of the Year and cited difficult parents as the primary reason ("Mass. HS. Basketball Coach", 2017). "At the end of the day, the reason I am resigning is because of parents. I don't want to deal with them," he said ("Mass. HS. Basketball Coach", 2017). Parents can constantly bother coaches about playing time for their athletes or write letters to the administration criticizing the coach or their methods and complaining about losses. Ultimately, parents can make it difficult for the coach to focus on the athletes' development. As Coach Castor stated, "...parents have taken the fun and enjoyment right out of it [coaching]-" ("Mass. HS. Basketball Coach", 2017).

What Controlling and Hovering Destroys

There are two main concerns with helicopter parenting or steamroller parenting. First and foremost, both possess the risk of destroying the parent-child relationship altogether. Many familial relationships have been negatively impacted by parental extremes. Often by the time the child has reached maturity, they rebel and/or seek significant distance–both physically and emotionally– from the extreme parent.

The second impact of extreme parenting is that it prevents the youth from establishing their own goals, succeeding or failing based on their own efforts— things that need to happen for them to effectively become independent adults. Extreme parents do not understand that growth and development come out of failure.

In Carol Dweck's book *Mindset*, the author addresses the results of shielding children from failure or adversity in relation to today's workforce (Dweck, 2006). Extreme parents who kept negativity at bay in the name of good parenting deprived their children, now adults, of the ability to persevere through daily challenges. We are currently faced with a workforce that includes young professionals in constant need of affirmation for any and all performance throughout their day. It's not uncommon for corporations to bring in consultants to help them navigate this issue; I can attest to this personally. Dweck eloquently sums it up by saying, "[Avoiding failure] is not a recipe for success in business, where taking on challenges, showing persistence, and admitting and correcting mistakes are essential-" (Dweck, 2006). If we don't let our kids learn from failure while they're young, success in the future will be hard to find.

Let's look at this in another way: Suppose you find a wild baby animal injured in the woods. You take that animal to a facility to be nursed back to health and provide for its every need until adulthood. The animal, upon release, has had no experience in an unprotected environment. What will happen when the animal needs to fend for itself in the natural habitat? Will that animal survive if you set it free after giving it food and warmth for most of its life? No, that animal will mostly fail to adapt to the wilderness.

Now a child is not a wild animal but think of it as a metaphor for what happens when a helicopter parent sends their child off into the world. Typically, that parent still suffocates the child until that child learns to fight for his or her independence. As an adult, the child is not as equipped to deal with the pitfalls of life as someone who was allowed to fail, guided through it, learned from it, and was inspired by it. Often, the adult who was shielded from all negativity during their developmental years, crumbles emotionally in the face of failure—they are ill prepared.

A friend and golf pro shared a story about a young golfer with whom he had difficulty coaching. The young man was a solid player and had a deep love for the game. However, the undermining factor in his success was his father's extreme parenting.

When the coach gave the player specific instructions, the father contradicted the coach's words, demanding the player do it his way. The coach asked the father not to purchase new equipment his son wasn't ready for, but the father did it anyway. Exhibiting his controlling behavior, this father parted ways with multiple coaches blaming each for his son's inability to grow as a player. As the young man entered adulthood, he not only walked away from the game, but he estranged himself from his father as well.

There was another extreme golf parent who desperately wanted his son to be successful in golf. The club to which they belonged had very few junior players. Of that small population of juniors, none played as well as this man's son, so the club put little to no effort into providing for junior events. One year, just before the annual club championship, this father approached the golf pro with an offer to pay for the club to purchase a trophy for the current year's junior event.

The caveat to this offer was that the father would require the club to engrave the son's name on the trophy for the prior two years. His son hadn't won the last two years. In fact, there was no junior championship those years because his son was the only one who signed up for it. Now, who benefits from this? Certainly not the son, who'd be receiving an accolade for something he didn't accomplish; that is counterproductive in fostering a solid work ethic, a growth mindset, and the grit necessary to overcome challenges on one's path to success in life. That father wasn't helping his athlete, just supporting his own ego and desires.

I had a client who was a Division I swimmer at a top school. This young man was personable, bright, and sensitive above all. Clearly, he was a talented swimmer, yet despite his talent, he left his sport and school after the first year.

Why? Well, after some time and some difficult events in his life, he came to see me. Eventually he came to admit to himself that it was his mother's constant hovering and obsessive control over him that made him choose to leave.

He recounted how, while in competition, if he swam poorly, he would receive his mother's recrimination. The minute he came out of the pool, he was met with her ire and disappointment. His anxiety over her admonishment grew to staggering levels and compelled him to walk away from a sport he loved.

He has just recently decided to go back to school but not to swim competitively. This was a direct avoidance of the parental pressure. Oddly enough, because he loves the sport, he has decided to turn his efforts to open water swimming. Open water swimming is swimming in the ocean, which, by nature, would exclude his mother from being present during competition—and pressure from her would be avoided.

Another client, a college golfer at an Ivy League school, walked off the course during a tournament and never returned because of the constant pressure from her father.

Not all who come to see me are youths with controlling parents. One in particular is a client who was a stellar football player from age 11 on. His parents were supportive, but they allowed him to pursue his path based on his own passion and grit. They were available to help, but never drove the proverbial bus. This athlete, now headed to Division I to play football, had a multitude of choices at his feet when it came time to play. This young man achieved his own success based on his own drive with the support and guidance of his parents. The extreme parent robs their athlete of self-assuredness, the development of grit, and learning how to persevere through difficulties. Whereas, parents who appropriately guide their child, as in the above example, will foster an environment that supports the development of a growth mindset, grit, and self-efficacy; all necessary for success in life.

What will the story be for your athlete? Go back to our discussion of external imaging. What would the camera see if it followed you and your child around every day? Are you a loving and supportive parent providing appropriate guidance and letting your child drive their own destiny? Or are you a hovering or controlling parent who does it for them? If you are the latter, and you think you're helping, think again.

Is Good Parenting Nature or Nurture?

In nature, animals instinctively know when to protect their young and when to let them use their instincts to survive on their own. However, it is my training and opinion that humans are not born with those same instincts. Human infants are the only infants on earth that have no instincts. Even when a baby nurses the sucking is merely a reflex; it is not instinct. Instead, everything a human does is learned. This leaves parents with the awesome responsibility of preparing their offspring for adulthood both physically and mentally.

An authoritative parent finds balance between having control and giving independence, while steamroller and helicopter parents control to the excess and squelch the child's development of independence. Though these two types of extreme parenting have different motives, the detriment they provide to the player are the same.

As a child grows physically, so too does their need for independence to foster their emotional growth. Despite intentions, it's all too easy for some parents to provide far too much protection or to control situations in an attempt to produce a positive outcome, inevitably hindering their child's emotional development.

Think back to when you were young and how you were given age-appropriate responsibilities like making your own bed, walking home from school, or getting a part-time job after school. These seemingly insignificant bits of independence and responsibility placed upon you as a child played a role in enabling you to be a functioning adult. All of them required your parents to 'let go' of some control.

Yet, so often now, I hear parents defend their excessive hovering, or even their need to control, stating they don't want their children to make mistakes or fail like they did. The parents believe they can ensure their child's success better than the child can.

I gently remind those parents to think about how those failures in their lives impacted their current successes. How mistakes or failures shaped the strong individual they are today or how those failures motivated them to do better and be better. Failure is necessary for anyone to grow and learn. I warn you: don't hover excessively or control situations to try and produce a certain outcome. Often, the results won't be what you anticipated and ultimately, you'll deprive your athlete of a growth experience.

Let's take another look at nature and how failure plays a role in growth. An example lies in muscle growth and myelin development.

By nature, muscles grow from failure. When muscles are exercised and worked beyond their ability, they tear. During periods of rest, muscles repair themselves. It is during the repair process that muscles grow and get stronger. This is why body builders will work out a specific set of muscles one day and a different set the next. Resting the previously worked muscles allows for their growth and development.

In his book, *Talent Code*, author Daniel Coyle explains that when athletes have deep-practice (as previously discussed), they are growing a crucial substance in their bodies called myelin—this process was previously called "muscle memory" (Coyle, 2009). He explains three crucial facts about myelin: "1 - Every human movement, thought, or feeling is a precisely timed electric signal traveling through a chain of neurons—a circuit of nerve fibers. 2 -Myelin is the insulation that wraps around these nerve fibers and increases signal strength, speed and accuracy. 3- The more we fire a particular circuit, the more Myelin optimizes that circuit and the stronger, faster, and more fluent our movements and thoughts become-" (Coyle, 2009).

To sum it up, the more we work at a particular skill, the more myelin grows. The more myelin, the better we are at performing because our circuits are firing off better, faster, and more accurately.

However, it's not a straight line to the top. As we've reiterated throughout this book: mistakes are necessary for growth to occur. Coyle (2009) writes, "Struggle is not optional—it's neurologically required: in order to get your skill circuit to fire optimally, you must by definition fire the circuit sub-optimally; you must make mistakes and pay attention to those mistakes; you must slowly teach your circuit. You must also keep firing your circuit— i.e. practicing—in order to keep Myelin functioning properly-" (Coyle, 2009).

Myelin and muscle growth are both examples of how nature positively responds to mistakes or failure. Yet, we as humans, often fear mistakes or failure, only placing value on success. But I am here to tell you that success is never achieved in the absence of failure along the way. It is out of mistakes that growth and development happen—with our bodies and minds. The growth, if sustained, will lead us toward success. Protecting your children from struggle robs them of many things, including chances to develop grit, self-efficacy, and the ultimate joy of success.

Are You an Extreme Parent?

As explained previously, if you hover or control and involve yourself in any and all aspects of your offspring's existence, allowing for little to no age-appropriate independence, then you can call yourself a helicopter or steamroller parent. Coming to this self-diagnosis requires a great deal of self-awareness on your part. Be honest with yourself and do some research. If your child is old enough, talk to him or her about how they perceive your parenting, ask other parents who have successfully raised strong adults how they did it and compare, or ask your child's health care professional for feedback.

An attorney who worked for a top international law firm told me that it was not uncommon to have new prospective recruits show up for an interview with one or more parents. When that happened, not only did it send red flags to the attorneys interviewing the candidates, but it practically eliminated them as prospects. Before you feel the need to hold a child's hand through a challenging event, ask yourself: Is this appropriate? Will my involvement hinder his or her ability to learn from this experience? Will my involvement cause others to view my athlete negatively?

There are distinct lines between the prudent parent and the extreme parent. To stay prudent, you'll need to make a significant amount of conscious decisions around when to protect and when to let go. Make sure you are giving your child age-appropriate freedom to learn and grow. Take into account your knowledge of your child's readiness for age-appropriate independence. You know your child better than anyone, so what may be appropriate for another child the same age as yours may not work for your child.

How Can You Stop Extreme Parenting?

If after reading this chapter, you realize you practice some extreme parenting behaviors, do not despair. Like so many things, this too can be fixed; the first step is recognition. Now that you have recognized it, take these steps:

1. Go back and reread the chapter on mindset to take note of growth-minded words. Use them every day in your vocabulary.

2. Place more age-appropriate responsibility on your child when they are ready for it: making their bed, walking to school, or getting a part-time job for example.

3. Change your conversations about schooling or athletics, so that they're two-way.

4. Have your child set goals for themselves. Let them feel the pain of unmet goals or the euphoria of their own achievements.

Independence and growth go hand in hand with success. If you want success for your child, then let them set their own goals, learn from their own mistakes, and excel based their own merits.

Remind yourself why you have them in sports—for the social, academic, physical, and emotional benefits. Extreme parenting jeopardizes these benefits from being realized by your athlete. Don't waste the opportunity sport provides because you are trying to force a result or experience for your child.

CHAPTER 11

Supporting From the Sidelines

Once my child was the one of the youngest golfers participating in the State Open. He made the cut on day one. On the second day, with 36 holes to play, the excitement started. My stomach was twisted in a knot, my throat was dry, and my hands were sweating—all before he placed the first ball on the tee. Several holes in and his game was on fire. He wasn't smiling, but I could see his walk, how he took his time, and addressed each shot. I knew he was happy. But that happy slowly slid off as he made one errant shot and then another. Each shot into fescue, or into the bunker just over the green, chipped away at him, and his clear focus was replaced with stress and frustration.

And although spectators are restricted from coaching, we were not restricted from encouraging the player. We could say "good shot" or "get your head back in the game," for example. Unfortunately, my "good shot" comments became, "Shake it off, get your head together, forget the last shot!" My angst skyrocketed with my athlete's and I sat, arms crossed in the golf cart, as my golfer went further and further in the hole. And by the second round of 18 holes that day, I finally stopped commenting. I could tell from his demeanor he had given up. And although he didn't end up all that bad score wise, he didn't play at his best and we knew it.

As much as I wanted to lecture on the way home, I refrained. He was beating himself up enough. And before we reached our first stop, he had calmed down and become reflective of his performance. All I could wonder was: *Where was that attitude when the wheels came off, and why weren't you listening to me? Did my being there help or hurt? Or, were my comments the problem? What do you need when this happens?*

Dr. Nick

During a seventh-grade baseball game, two fathers are coaching a team of boys. The team is losing and one of the coaches' sons gets called out. He throws his bat down in frustration. The father of the son who loses his cool immediately extracts his son physically from the field and holds him against the fence. The father gets in his son's face and starts screaming at him inches from his son's face, just out of sight of the parents in the stands.

As this parent is viciously reprimanding his child, the other coach sees and comes over and addresses him.

"Don't tell me how to parent my own child!" the angry parent/coach retorts.

"I don't care how you parent, but I do care how you come across to our players and their parents. If anyone sees you exploding on a player like this there will be an uproar. Deal with it later, on your own time!"

The angry parent relents and later apologizes to the other coach for losing his cool. Let's face it, life stresses and constant demands on our time can add up. One little stressor can send the best of us over the edge. Now in this case, this father and coach was a known "hothead" but the reason for me retelling this story is to examine the situation as a whole.

The first fact: the child showed error in judgment. The second fact: the error needed correction. The child needed to understand that he demonstrated bad sportsmanship and should not repeat such an action. The question becomes: Was the way this father/coach handled it correct, damaging, or necessary? Did the punishment fit the crime?

I heard this story from the point of view of the coach who stepped in, who so logically told me, "I coach my son's baseball teams because I love doing it. I'm a dad first and foremost, except when we are on that field in practice or during a game. I have a responsibility to not only my child but to every child playing and I have made that fact clear to my son. That said, how I reprimand the players is as even across the board as it can possibly be. If someone is taken out of the game for bad sportsmanship, then they can explain it to their parents, and I have had to do that. It is in fact part of the learning process and will ultimately make the kids better players, team-mates, and individuals in life overall." The first coach goes on to say that he would never tell anyone how to punish or admonish their child, but in this case when he saw the other coach being so harsh to one of the players, he felt he needed to step in. I happen to agree with him.

The angered coach in this story clearly mishandled the situation; however, his need to react was on point. Because the player was wrong in throwing his bat in anger, he needed to be corrected to learn and grow as a player and an individual. However, his father's force and over-the-top physical and verbal aggression ruined that outcome. Fear and recrimination may have made the father feel better, but it did nothing to teach the child. Instilling fear will never work as a motivator, but it will cause a player to become riddled with self-doubt and anxiety, neither of which is a key element in achieving excellence in anything.

Conversely, let's suppose the angry coach simply ignored or covered up his son's infraction and never mentioned it. Would that have been appropriate or better? No. In fact, not handling it is just as egregious and detrimental to the player as handling it too harshly. Both extremes remove the learning and growth opportunities from the experience and harm the player for their future performances.

How does this story relate to "supporting from the sidelines?" First, it helps me make it clear that no matter your role in the event—coach, parent, or both—you are still there to support the players. Second, it gives me the opportunity to establish what I mean by sidelines. Sidelines can be at the game or practice or anywhere you and the athlete are discussing his or her performance: in the car, at home, and so on. And lastly, this story shows that how you support from the sidelines, as a parent or coach, can impact your player or other players—at times significantly.

As a parent and psychologist, I completely understand the hurt that comes when your child is struggling and the stress that develops when your child is frustrated and about to give up. I also understand the anger that comes when your player's behavior during the game is disappointing, as it was in the previous story. The intrinsic desire to rescue them and solve their problem is innate in parents. Yet, even though this internal need to protect is instinctual, it will hinder a child's ability to learn and grow, which is essential to becoming a successful adult.

When watching a soccer game, swim meet, track meet, or hockey tournament, you will never eradicate the multitude of annoyances, like rude parents or ineffective coaches. Instead, it's how you deal with these situations that matters for the sake of your athlete or athletes. Remember, how we nurture their mental game influences their physical performance.

Well-known life coach, author, and entrepreneur, Anthony Robbins eloquently stated in his book *Awaken the Giant Within*, "It's in the moments of decision that your destiny is shaped-" (Robbins, 1991). Could that be taken further to say parents' decisions shape the destinies of our children? Yes, absolutely. Parents are the greatest influencers of their children. Parental decisions regarding their own behavior while supporting from the sidelines directly impact an athlete's performance.

If our choices ultimately affect our destinies and those of our athletes, then we must first see why we make the choices we do. Everything we do has a purpose and there are two basic factors that drive that purpose: avoiding negative feelings and gaining positive feelings.

You brush your teeth to avoid cavities; you go to work to have nice things and to avoid financial hardship; you work out to feel good and/or to avoid feeling tired or gaining weight. Everything we do has a purpose and that primary purpose is to avoid the bad and acquire the good. This concept is most effectively explained by Anthony Robbins, where he defines this as the "pain-pleasure principle" (Robbins, 1991).

That is why some parents get angry at other parents, coaches, or our athletes. They think showing their disapproval or frustration will change the outcome of a poor athletic performance. They try to shift the experience to avoid pain and gain pleasure.

Based on the fact that all behavior is purpose driven, there is a theory purported by Prescott Lecky (1945), who was a lecturer of Psychology at Columbia University from 1924 to 1934. Lecky theorized that individuals are internally driven to maintain consistency in their behavior—they behave certain ways on purpose. Lecky called this the Theory of Self Consistency. He said, in order to maintain the consistency, the individual has to develop a "master motive."

Lecky explains the "master motive" as a set of ideas, ideals, or core values. An individual uses this "master motive" to keep their behavior in check and consistent (Lecky, 1945). Ask yourself what is your "master motive?" What guides your behavior toward consistency?

Let's look at this theory in regards to parenting a young athlete. Ask yourself: what would make being on the sideline as pleasurable as possible for you? What would make it best for your child? Would that mean mindfulness—being in the moment and blocking everything else out? What about self-regulation and identifying stress triggers for you and your athlete? Appropriate behavior both on and off the field?

Parents tend to be keenly focused on what their athlete needs to bring to any practice, scrimmage, tournament, or championship game. Parents quite often shout instructions like "Stay focused!", "Ignore negative comments!", "Remember your goals!" Yet, as they park the car and head to the sidelines, parents are often ill-equipped to be the supporters their athlete desperately needs them to be.

People usually overinflate or underinflate the role of parenting in their athlete's achievement of excellence. Both approaches are detrimental to any athlete, creating potentially harmful results including feeling intense pressure and feeling completely unsupported. That's why I always tell parents: before you take your child to any event or practice where you plan to be on the sidelines, set goals for yourself. Determine your "master motive."

Yes, parents need to set goals for themselves as they carry out the important role of supporting from the sidelines. Yet before we can set any goal, parents must understand what support means to the athlete. Like a pillar supports a structure, the parent must hold up and be the strength their athlete can emotionally lean on. Whether the athlete fails to bring their "A game" or they nail it that day, the parent needs to absorb the resulting emotions and keep the athlete emotionally on track.

These goals, however, need time and open communication to establish. Do not wait until you're on the way to the championship game to say to your child something like, "Dad's not going to yell from the stands today." Establishing goals is best done long before the game. Choose a quiet, calm time for you and your athlete to discuss your goals and establish them together. Remember the three levels of goal setting during this process: Outcome, performance, and process—this process should be the same as the one your child uses to set their own goals.

But before you have that conversation with your athlete and start establishing your goals, as a parent you need to self-reflect on your own values. You also need to acknowledge your own triggers—what sets you off with other parents, coaches, and athletes? And finally, there should be a moment when you as a parent answer, "When I lose it, how will it affect—or how has it affected—my child during the game, after the game, at school, or elsewhere?" Remember Newton's third law: "For every action, there is an equal and opposite reaction-" ("Newtons Third Law", n.d.). Every time you lose it at the game, your child will hear about it from their coach, friends, or competitors. How will your child feel? Is that what you want for your child? How will that change how your child views you and will they emulate your behavioral choices?

Of course, answering this multitude of questions will require one thing: empathy. In a previous chapter, we discussed imagery and the athlete's ability to visualize themselves internally and externally. Internally is how the athlete sees things and externally is how the athlete looks as if their action were being filmed by a camera. When pondering their actions on the sidelines, I encourage parents to take the time to use imagery to assess what you want your own behavior to look like—both internally and externally—then set goals accordingly.

I work quite often in the golf industry with many junior golfers who play competitively. More than a few times, I have witnessed the hovering parent on the practice green, dictating instructions right before that child is called to the event's first tee. I can usually feel the angst emanating from the athlete at the moment when the child needs support the most.

As a result of your words and actions, your athlete should feel certain that your love and support does not depend on their performance on the playing field. Do not tie love with performance. I am sure many who read the prior statement think, "Oh I don't do that." But are you sure? It's more common than you think. Put yourself in an empathetic state and see how your actions and words are seen through your athlete's eyes.

Once, I had a young athlete whose father believed his love was never tied to performance. But his tone and body language on the course told me otherwise. The player conveyed this to me as well. A bad day of play meant yelling, hurtful comments, and being shunned by his dad. Conversely, on a good day of play, his father embellished him with over-the-top praise and affection. What his athlete saw and felt was, *I get my father's love when I play well.*

After self-reflection, take the time to ask your child what bothers them. What are their triggers with you on the sidelines? Perhaps you will be surprised at the answers. The actions and words you perceive as supportive may actually add to the stress level of the athlete. Talking openly and honestly with your athlete will give you more insight and help you set your goals as a spectator. This will allow both you and your athlete to enjoy future events with greater success.

Succumbing to Provocation

Imagine you walk onto the bleachers, goals in your head, and you are all set to be the most incredible parent on the sidelines. But somewhere in the mess of parents, you hear a negative comment from a consistently annoying parent, directed at your player. How do you stick to your goals, and not turn around and let this guy have it?

Controlling an immediate reaction to an emotional trigger is one of the hardest things to do. Someone accuses you of wrongdoing and you want to verbally attack your accuser. A driver cuts you off on the road and you want to go after them. We face a million of these emotional triggers each day. Why do we fall for some and resist others? How do you stop being a reactionary person?

At any point of change in your mood, you have 90 seconds to turn it around before the new feeling begins to fester. If you don't stop the feeling within 90 seconds, it will go on for three to seven minutes, and ultimately longer, if you don't stop it in that short period of time (Taylor, 2006).

So, how do you turn it around in 90 seconds? You use imagery to counteract an unwanted emotion—specifically a reciprocal image. If you replace a negative image with a positive image, you can immediately calm your anger.

Let's suppose another parent just yelled something negative from the stands about your child's performance. This parent has been a thorn in your side for a long time and your temper is flaring. All you can think about is turning around and verbally assaulting the windbag. What do you do? Like I said, you have 90 seconds to turn it around. Immediately, take that image of you verbally defending your child, and replace it with a thought of you and your child going out for ice cream after the game, for example. Any happy or calming thought can bring your head around within that 90 second window.

Remember, your brain is incapable of holding a negative image and a positive image at the same time (Garavan, 1998). To eradicate the negative thought—the one invoked by an annoying parent, your player missing a shot, or whatever else triggers you—you have 90 seconds to replace that negative thought with a positive one. Predetermine that positive thought before the game so you are ready to use it if necessary. Once you have successfully done that, you have kept your emotions in check and stopped the escalation of anger, potentially harming your player's emotional and physical performance.

As you set your goals, perform external imagery and see what the camera would see when you are sitting on the sidelines. What would you want your player to see: a parent who is understanding and supportive? This external image will help you self-regulate. So too, will having your mental reciprocal prompt ready to go when you feel like abandoning your goals.

As parents, our actions can at times be quite harmful, even though we are mostly well meaning. Ultimately, make your goal to inspire your athlete. Don't be a distraction that negatively affects their performance. The first step is open, honest communication to discover what those triggers are for both sides. Establish your goals, measure them often (ask your child), and adjust your processes until you find one that works for you. Remember, goal setting as I said before is iterative, and modifications are likely, but you need to persevere for your athlete, as well as for your own enjoyment and well-being.

Mindfulness

British philosopher Allan Watts said, "You don't dance to get to the other side of the floor-" (Watts, n.d.). This quote speaks to the concept of mindfulness: being present in the moment and truly experiencing what is occurring right then. Why is this so important for supporting your athletes?

In society today we are so caught up in technology and the increased ability to multitask that we often fail to live in the moment and experience. We do something new and exciting, but we are often too busy trying to post our experience to the world that we don't fully enjoy it. We often fail to emotionally connect with the people we're with because of all the technological distractions—including times when your athletes need you to be experiencing what they are. Support means guiding, choosing the right words, and being 100% present in the moment.

For example, you head to the game with a goal to watch your child calmly, without getting caught up in other parents' annoying discussions—often centering around your child's performance. Your goal is set. You make it through the first thirty minutes, when your child misses a catch and the parent next to you makes a snarky comment. You use the reciprocal imagery we talked about within 90 seconds, and you stop yourself from reacting negatively towards this parent. You give yourself a deserved pat on the back.

Your phone buzzes. You take a look to see who just sent you a text and you are compelled to reply. But as you do this, your athlete catches the ball this time, throws the ball to second base and manages two outs. You completely miss it. Have you been mindful?

In this scenario, you the parent achieved your goal, and harm from a bad reaction was thwarted, but by not being completely mindful and being pulled away by your phone, you missed an important moment your child will want to discuss later.

If we are not present and acknowledging what is going on around us, including how we are reacting to something negative or experiencing fully the moment we are in, we can't adjust our behavior for the benefit of our children. Be mindful and give of yourself fully for an experience—being present completely is for the benefit of your athlete and yourself.

I understand the demands of the world we live in completely and that some interruptions are inevitable, but the more mindful we become as supporters of our children, the more supported they will feel—which directly impacts their mental game.

Active Listening

Parents insist to me all the time that they are listening to their athletes and that they know what they want or need. Truthfully, some do, but there are many that fall short of listening. In order to be a good listener, you have to *hear* what the person is saying. Again, let's revisit being mindful–be present in the moment. Clearly, I am not talking about the physical act, but the act of absorbing what is really being said beyond the words.

Effective listening may require the parent to be able to read the child's body language. You know your child best, so watch how they answer a question as well as hear the words they use. It's the body movements, the eyes, and the tone that say more than the sentence uttered. Ask questions often—again, without judging their answers—and give them time to respond. The conversational goal must be truth even if it's not what you as a parent want to hear, and in order for that to occur, your child needs to feel you will hear what they say without judgment or offense.

Once we can effectively listen to our athletes, we can provide the guidance in directing them toward their goals and desires. One of the most effective teaching methods can be modeling. The more we demonstrate and live our own lives according to what we teach, the greater chance our children have to absorb those qualities.

Let them see you set goals and achieve them or even fail, but then correct your failures. Children mimic our behaviors knowingly but mostly unknowingly, which makes a huge argument for parents to behave as we want our children to behave.

Non-Verbal Cues

During competition, it's difficult to accurately assess how your child is doing emotionally. Still, the mental game is the most critical aspect of sports and determining their state during competition can be difficult. Therefore, prior to any competition, address this issue with your athlete. Discuss clues to send each other without even making eye contact. It could be any physical gesture that no one else would pick up on, such as touching their forehead as if they were removing sweat or wringing their hands like they are getting ready for the next play. This may ease the stress of both parent and player.

Dealing with Other Parents

Every sporting event, no matter the level or intensity, carries a certain spirit—a level of regard or a sense of value. Ideally, the spirit should be of regard modeled for and by all the individuals present. When we have regard for something, we value it, respect it, and generally act accordingly. Unfortunately, more often than not, the spirit of competition rules, and it manifests itself in a negative energy emanated from many of the parents, often transcending the stands and infecting the playing field.

When I work with athletes and their parents, particularly at a higher level, I discuss from a mental aspect the need for regard. I focus on the athlete and parents having regard—value and respect—for themselves as well as for other players and parents. It's when we lose the sense of regard that we behave in a way that's conducive to negativity.

Have you ever observed that parent or parents that everyone gravitates toward? Or the player that everyone loves for more than their athletic prowess? Typically, those individuals have a high level of regard. They stand out because of how they carry themselves and the behavior they display during good and bad times. Those individuals represent the behavior we should mimic as supporters from the sidelines.

Intrinsically, when we demonstrate a spirit of regard, we can absorb negative criticism with grace. We actively listen and model the behavior we want our athletes to show on the field and off. As a parent and supporter of your athlete, you have a responsibility to ensure your behavior breeds a sense of value toward others and their opinions.

Is this an easy task to achieve when you are hearing negative comments hurled in the direction of your athlete? No, it's almost impossible not to lash-out at the offender, but you have to hold it in. As your athlete's biggest supporter, you need to not react to the jealousy and meanness of other parents. Many parents attempt to insulate themselves from the negative spirit of competition, but it inevitably will get to you at some point. The only thing you can control in these situations is your own reaction. Make sure you don't react to the mean spirit with a vicious counterattack. Counterattacks increase your anxiety and they will inevitably be seen by your athlete and affect their performance. Learn to absorb and move away from the offenders—remember the 90 second rule.

You need to be the model version of behavior you want and expect to see from your child. How can you ask or demand them to behave a certain way if you don't live up to your own standards?

Dealing with the Coach

Coaches come in many forms and have different levels of expertise. Whether your child is being coached by a classmate's dad or by a top-level professional, the parental behavior should be the same: you should respect your child's coach. Parents should regard—a.k.a. value—their child's coach no matter if they agree with him or her or not. That's because you expect the same respectful behavior from your child. I think most would agree that we want our children to respect their coaches.

Will there be times you disagree with the coach? Absolutely. But a respectful conversation off the playing field is the only place to address differences of opinion. If you feel you need to let them out, remember to show respect. To do that, you need to be an active listener. Express your concerns and then really hear what the coach is saying. Even if your mind doesn't change, you must show the coach the respect they deserve.

In other words, do not yell at the coach from the sidelines, or say nasty comments to them at any time. Others are watching, particularly the athletes, and this will undermine their efforts and hinder the results of the day's play. All sporting events are about the athletes participating, not about what the parents feel the coaches should do or not do. Disagreement should only be expressed through calm, rational, private conversation where active listening is present.

If you are confronted with a coach who spends a significant amount of time belittling and/or yelling at your athlete or the team as a whole, it can feel impossible to watch and ignore. But resist the urge to confront them in front of other players or other parents. All conversations should be done privately as to avoid putting either party in a bad light or on the defensive.

The best way to avoid putting the coach on the defensive is to begin the private conversation by calmly asking the following two questions:

"Where do you believe my athlete needs to improve and what specifically should they do?"

"What can we do to help?"

These two questions typically disarm the coach and take him or her off the defensive by making the coach feel respected, not undermined. This is important for the conversation to be productive. Once you have started the talk on this positive note, then you can address their coaching methods on the field—the true reason you requested the meeting. At this point, however, tone of voice is critical. It's imperative for a productive conversation to remain calm and nonjudgmental in your tone as you deliver the following two questions:

"How do you think my athlete feels when you yell at him or her like that?"

"How do you think I feel when you yell at my child like that?"

Typically, when you ask someone how they feel about a certain situation they caused, they will do anything to avoid answering. The coach, in this instance, will evade the question by giving explanations defending their actions—they will go on the defensive. At this point, remain calm and respectful in your tone, re-ask the same question:

"I don't think you understood my question. I asked, 'How do you think my athlete feels when you talk to him or her like that?'"

If the coach keeps going back to avoidance and defensiveness, keep asking the same question. Eventually the coach will be forced to answer and will have to face the truth of his or her actions. This will induce a more thoughtful coaching method, if only to avoid having to discuss this with you or another parent later on.

As with any difficult conversation, go in with the goal of remaining calm. Even if the coach gets heated, keep your patience in check by imagining your child was there watching. Think of how they would perceive your behavior because if you lose it in the meeting, there is a good chance your behavior will somehow make it back to the team.

But what if your child wants to approach their coach on their own? Let's suppose you're angry with the coach but then your child comes to you also unhappy about the same situation. And suppose they tell you they want to confront the coach on their own. Do you let them or tell them you will handle it?

In these situations, I always tell parents to determine the intent first. The intent should be to either inform the coach respectfully or to learn. The intent should never be to criticize. As a parent, how you approach this with your child is crucial. You must be sure of the intent, then role play with your child. This role playing should focus on respect at all times while making the intent of the conversation evident. This teaches the child how to approach others with respect and an open mind—rather than attacking out of emotion. Remember parents, you are the greatest influence in your child's life. They learn from the examples you set, so make sure they learn the right lessons for them to achieve success in life.

Do's and Don'ts

Too many times we have witnessed or heard of a parent approaching the coach, a referee, or a player with ire and public admonishment. It's gotten so bad that many high schools draft pre-season expectation letters describing proper and improper parental behavior at sporting events. Some community fields have posted signs establishing rules for sideline behavior. It's a sad truth about the world we live in, that adults need reminders how to behave at sporting events.

I think the first thing any and all parents need to remember is that the event is the child's and the child's alone. Parents need to remember why they signed their athlete up for that sport in the first place. Sports are for developing the child physically, emotionally, and socially. Does the child gain anything when their parent is unruly at their game? No, in fact the child loses a great deal when Mom or Dad can't behave like an adult. They can face ridicule or be shunned by other players, coaches, and even parents.

Again, I press upon you to be mindful in the presence of your child. Feel your emotions without judging and consciously choose to cast aside the ineffective negative thoughts—they will only cause additional pressure and potentially cause your athlete to do less than their best. Your anger or frustration may be justified but ask yourself if expressing it will help or hurt your present situation.

You are an integral part of your child achieving athletic success but perhaps not the way you think. Many parents believe that they need to express every thought they have when they have it to inspire their child to do better. Others believe that accolades deserved or not are the way to get success from the child. As I've stated multiple times throughout this book, neither is true or effective.

Also, children are as in tune to their parents as their parents are to them. So even if you don't say a word, they can read every look, every facial nuance with laser precision. Think long and hard about how you react on the sidelines, during the car ride home, or at dinner, and how it plays into your child's athletic performance.

Hold yourself to a high standard of respect and regard, and avoid the traps set by others to bait you into being the worst version of yourself in front of your child and others. Remember your "master motive" to maintain a strong, consistent behavior that will set a positive example for everyone around you.

In July 2017, professional golfer, Kenny Perry, won the Senior U.S. Open. As I watched Kenny walk off the 18th green and hug his wife, I heard the commentators give their praise for his polished performance both on and off the course. For every accolade on his golf skills, there were equal if not more positive comments about who he is as a person. One commentator professed what a nice guy he is and explained that he never says a bad word about anyone. He said that for all the years Kenny's been playing the game, every player that talks about him only has nice things to say.

What does that story have to do with parenting from the sidelines? Well, let's go back to the Theory of Self-Consistency by Preston Lecky. Lecky told us that individuals have a "master motive" or set of ideas, ideals, or values by which they conduct themselves. Clearly, Kenny Perry possesses values and ideals consistent with how he handles himself on and off the golf course. He is an example of someone who should be emulated.

If we want to produce young athletes with a sense of good sportsmanship, parents need to be the models for that. Parents are responsible for setting those values and following them themselves as a means of instilling them—especially while watching from the sidelines.

Every day presents an opportunity for excellence; will you achieve it for the betterment of your child? Is it worth it to you? Only you can answer those questions but think about them the next time you are ready to scream at a coach or make a nasty comment to an annoying parent sitting beside you. *How do I want to be perceived by others, especially my child?*

CHAPTER 12

Let Them Play

The tree's decorated, snow is falling softly outside, your stereo murmurs a quiet soothing carol as you open your front door to grab the mail. You hold the stack of holiday cards in your hand and breathe deeply. The mail is littered with cards depicting the perfect, happy family on vacation in some remote paradise or on a snowy mountain as they swish down the slopes—all appearing like models in a magazine. You smile, knowing the stack you sent out the day before aren't that different. But then as you flip, you come to one family's annual letter:

"Oh, what a year we've had!... Molly is excelling in the math and science arena, Harrison is fast becoming a track star, and our newest addition to the family, Fluffy, is the most perfect dog, ever!..."

You roll your eyes because you know from the family gossip mill: Molly is failing English and Harrison hates running track and plans to quit next season and Fluffy recently attacked the neighbor's cat and they're suing for damages.

What would happen if we all abandoned this incredible need to be perfect? What if we didn't put on a front for the world that we are the perfect parents, that our kids are all amazing, and that our lives are straight out of a movie? What if we stopped posting all the "perfect" things our kids do all the time on Facebook and Instagram? What if our lives were openly as messy as they really are?

Recently, a friend reminded me of a YouTube video called "Hockey Canada PSA Relax, It's just a game GOLF." In the video, a man is putting on a green with his golf buddies watching. The camera widens, and his kid is standing next to him taunting him not to screw up, reminding him that it's important that he do well, and saying other things parents are known to say. Besides being humorous, the video is clearly designed for parents to see themselves through their child's eyes—that empathetic look that Dr. Nick discussed earlier. If you haven't watched it, then Google it; I can assure you it will hit home. Inevitably, my hope is for you to be doing some of the empathy tasks Dr. Nick has instructed you to do in this book.

But if you stop and think about it and really ponder what is underneath the message of the video, you'll realize it really shows what sports parents have become. It's a harsh reality of the pressure we put on our kids to be better than us, to master everything they touch—a constant push toward perfectionism. And what happens when all the hoopla of youth sports dies and your kids are older and not playing sports professionally? Will you sit back and regret the time, feel like you or they failed, or will you see it for what it was: preparation for life?

Once the equipment becomes another thing to reorganize, donate, or dust, nostalgia takes over and we ask: "Was it worth all the time, money, car rides, and stress? After all, what was the point?" Not long after my son placed his clubs in the closet, did I come to realize what he really received from playing golf. Golf had been his vehicle to developing a strong sense of self, grace, and character.

Nowadays, my once pristinely dressed golfer is donning a fireman's suit and helmet. His hours practicing at the golf course have been replaced by hours at the firehouse or on the fire truck training and responding to emergencies. I'd be lying if I said my heart doesn't jump every time his pager goes off and he flies out the door. But while one could look back and say, "What a waste; he was such a good golfer," I instead say, "Thank God for the emotional strength he got from competing in golf all those years. The emotional strength, mental fortitude, and character have given him the ability to pursue his passion in helping others as a first responder." It was never about him being perfect, but about working toward his own excellence in whatever passion he had.

Dr. Nick

If I were to choose the most important take-away from this book, I would be hard pressed to narrow it down to one thing. But one of the greatest and most significant ideas for parents and coaches to understand is: an athlete will never master the basics. Really, no matter your level in sports, you should always be practicing the basics. Why is this crucial? Because it should be understood that participation in sports is a constant "learn and grow" proposition. No one ever reaches perfection. Perfection or mastery is no more attainable in sport than it is any other area of life.

Now, I am sure the previous statements have some of you screaming at this book in denial, but ultimately you must accept this fact. The goal of any athlete should never be mastery, but to get to their highest level. Personal excellence should be the goal.

Sport is an iterative process composed of failures and successes. If your athlete learns how to navigate and utilize sport as a rich environment of developing mental strength, they will be an unstoppable force in every area of life they choose. The open-minded, gritty, efficacious person understands this dynamic in depth: failure is an opportunity to grow and success is the reward of hard work and never giving up.

Before the Philadelphia Eagles won the Super Bowl in 2018 with Nick Foles as the quarterback, they were the underdogs to the ultimate rivals: the New England Patriots and Tom Brady. In his post-game interviews, Nick Foles' demeanor projected a humbled, respectful individual who ultimately knew how he became the man he is (Trinko, 2018). He wasn't filled with delusions of perfection or superiority. Instead he attributed his current success to all the times he failed. He knew that having failures gave him opportunities to learn and grow (Trinko, 2018). Foles embodies growth mindedness.

Foles discussed having come close to giving up his dream of a professional football career when he wasn't playing well. But he stuck with it, eventually landing on the Kansas City Chiefs. Foles kept practicing the basics and moving forward. Becoming the first backup quarterback in 16 years to win the Super

Bowl was not his goal; achieving personal excellence in a game he loved was (Trinko, 2018).

As a society, we get so caught up in being perfect and showing no flaws that we place unnecessary emotional pressures on ourselves and our young athletes. Stop. Perfection is unattainable and should never be the goal. If you focus on achieving something beyond human reach you will fail to win. Your closed-minded approach will deter any learning from failure. Ultimately, this will leave you emotionally defeated.

I chuckle when I hear people criticize a pro-athlete for failing to perform a basic skill. Whether they fail to catch a pass or hit an errant shot or miss the simplest of blocks, we are quick to judge from the comforts of our homes. Yet, when we watch any athlete, whether they are children, professional, or Olympians the error made always relates to a basic skill. In my opinion, no one ever masters the basic skills of sport at the 100% level. If that was possible, then why would high level athletes continue to practice and be coached? Therefore, in my work with high level athletes, I always address that performing basic skills requires intense effort and that one should do so without defending the probability of an error occurring which is not within their control limit.

Early on, we discussed how youth sports have changed over the years. How it went from a small pastime to the all-consuming business it is today. But sports have also changed how we parent and how we as parents spend our free time. Many families with young children spend most of their weekends shuttling kids to and from athletic activities. Quite often families center their free time around athletic events and the pressure for their athletes to perform is ever present.

We see our kids as extensions of ourselves, and many parents live vicariously through their children. If they play a sport that the parent loves, it is a way to connect. But that connection can sometimes manifest itself into the very thing that forces them apart because of parental pressure. As a society, we have raised athletics to such heights that our kids aren't always reaping the emotional benefits that sports provide.

A friend and coach told me once that when he counsels parents on the sidelines he says, "Let *them* play. Let *them* learn. It's the best thing you can do for them."

Recently, I turned on ABC's Good Morning America. The news anchors were discussing Robin Roberts' college basketball career and how well she played. Roberts said that although she never made a career of basketball, her time playing ball was a significant reason why she went on to have such a successful career. She added that her coworkers also have the ability to do their jobs at such a high level because of their experience playing sports. The intrinsic value of sports cultivates and creates a mentally strong individual leading to success in life. Roberts basically summed up the whole reason we have written this book—using sports can be a teaching vehicle for high performance in sport and in life.

One of my true passions in life is working with athletes of all ages to improve their mental game and subsequently see their physical performances reach new heights. It never fails to amaze me how so many athletes, parents, and coaches overlook the power of the mind. They discount the effects the mind has on the physical game. However, it has been proven time and time again that you can be the most physically prepared athlete but, without a strong mental game, you will never achieve performance excellence.

This is why I call the mind "the athlete's powerhouse." The mind is the overall controller—it is the central processor for all movement. Discounting its importance or failing to develop it is a mistake and limiting to all athletes. But once developed, the athletic powerhouse will deliver the athlete a set of skills that transcends athletics and produces a successful performer in every area of their lives.

In athletics and many other areas of life, there is a traditional path to success and an unconventional path. There is no one way that works for everyone. However, the attributes discussed in this book are essential for whatever path your athlete takes. As a parent or coach, it's crucial for you to read your athlete and know what they are saying with and without words: Are they burned out? Does this path work for them? Are they ready for a change? Are they capable of taking on more?

This book is designed to assist a parent or coach, starting with the most important aspect of nurturing a young athlete: knowing who they are and what their temperament is. Knowing your athlete is critical to aid you in fostering important attributes such as mindset, grit, self-efficacy, goal setting, and practice. Kids are not exactly alike in how they process information and how you, as an adult, foster these attributes will differ from child to child.

Once you know yourself and how you approach life, once you know your athlete and how they receive information, then you can begin to address the attributes we've presented. As I have said multiple times, instilling these necessary qualities in your athlete can last for a lifetime, but it takes time and patience. Maintaining consistency and repetition during teachable moments will embed the positive attributes in your athlete. They will naturally transfer what they have learned through athletics to every area of their life.

We need to remember that sports are a vehicle to learn the attributes that inspire excellence in performance. Not every youth athlete wants to be a professional or play in college, and yet the takeaways these casual players have are the same as those of the athletes that achieve high levels of success. They learn social skills, how to deal with adversity, and what it means to work hard to achieve goals. Use sports to reinforce these critical lessons for success. I hope this book can help guide you on that mission to making your child or the child you coach mentally strong and able to reach all their goals, whatever they may be.

INDEX

Intro

19 Miner, Julianna W. (2016, June 1). Why 70 Percent of Kids Quit Sports by Age 13. Retrieved from https://www.washingtonpost.com

Chapter 1:

28 Mgbemere, Bianca and Telles, Rachel (2013, December 11). Types of Parenting Styles and How to Identify Yours/Developmental Psychology at Vanderbilt. Retrieved from https://my.vanderbilt.edu/developmentalpsychology/2013/12/page/2/ 28

28 Mgbemere, Bianca and Telles, Rachel (2013, December 11). Types of Parenting Styles and How to Identify Yours/Developmental Psychology at Vanderbilt. Retrieved from https://my.vanderbilt.edu/developmentalpsychology/2013/12/page/2/

29 Mgbemere, Bianca and Telles, Rachel (2013, December 11). Types of Parenting Styles and How to Identify Yours/Developmental Psychology at Vanderbilt. Retrieved from https://my.vanderbilt.edu/developmentalpsychology/2013/12/page/2/

29-30 Mgbemere, Bianca and Telles, Rachel (2013, December 11). Types of Parenting Styles and How to Identify Yours/Developmental Psychology at Vanderbilt. Retrieved from https://my.vanderbilt.edu/developmentalpsychology/2013/12/page/2/

30 Mgbemere, Bianca and Telles, Rachel (2013, December 11). Types of Parenting Styles and How to Identify Yours/Developmental Psychology at Vanderbilt. Retrieved from https://my.vanderbilt.edu/developmentalpsychology/2013/12/page/2/

32 The New York Longitudinal Study Alexander Thomas, Stella Chess, Herbert G. Birch personality types – temperament traits. Retrieved from https://www.age-of-the-sage.org/psychology/chess_thomas_birch.html

32-33 The New York Longitudinal Study Alexander Thomas, Stella Chess, Herbert G. Birch personality types – temperament traits. Retrieved from https://www.age-of-the-sage.org/psychology/chess_thomas_birch.html

33-34 The New York Longitudinal Study Alexander Thomas, Stella Chess, Herbert G. Birch personality types – temperament traits. Retrieved from https://www.age-of-the-sage.org/psychology/chess_thomas_birch.html

35 Understanding "Goodness of Fit." Retrieved from https://centerforparentingeducation.org

35 Sansone, A.V., Hemphill, S.A., and Smart, D. (2004). Connections between temperament and social development: A review. Social Development, 13(1), 142-170.

36-37 Rajaratnam, A.C. & Garcias, A. (n.d.). Finding the Right Parenting Style to Match Your Child's Temperament. Retrieved from https://www.parentcircle.com

37 Thomas, A. & Chess, S. (1977). Temperament and development. Brunner/Mazel.

37 Bates, J.E., Schermerhorn, A.C., Petersen, I.T., Zentner, M., & Shiner, R. (2012). Handbook of temperament.

37 Thomas, A. & Chess, S. (1977). Temperament and development. Brunner/Mazel.

38 Thomas, A. & Chess, S. (1977). Temperament and development. Brunner/Mazel.

38 Sansone, A.V., Hemphill, S.A., and Smart, D. (2004). Connections between temperament and social development: A review. Social Development, 13(1), 142-170.

Chapter 2:

41 Dweck, Carol S. (2006) Mindset, 1st. ed., New York, NY.: Random House, Inc.

41 Spears, Marc J. (2017, February 16). Isaiah Thomas Journey from Final Draft to NBA All-Star. Retrieved from https://www.Theundefeated.com

41 *"All I wanted was a chance"*, Ibid. 2

42 Spears, Marc J. (2017, February 16). Isaiah Thomas Journey from Final Draft to NBA All-Star. Retrieved from https://www.Theundefeated.com

42-43 Roenigk, Alyssa via ESPN (2018, February 14). Shaun White Signs off to YOLO to Spark Tears and Relief

44 Dweck, Carol S. (2006), Ibid.

45 Dweck, Carol S. (2006), Ibid.

45 *"…when things are safely within their grasp. When things get too challenging, when they're not feeling smart or talented, or they lose interest."*: Ibid, 22

46 Dweck, Carol S. (2006), Ibid.

47 *"…effort can reduce you.",* Ibid. 42

47 Dweck, Carol S. (2006), Ibid.

48 (2015, October 17). Newsweek Special Edition, Jordan: 30 Years Since MJ Changed the Game. Retrieved from https://www.newsweek.com

48 *"Whenever I was working out and got tired and figured I ought to stop, I'd close my eyes and see that list in the locker room without my name on it,"* Jordan would explain. *"That usually got me going again."* (2015, October 17). Newsweek Special Edition, Jordan: 30 Years Since MJ Changed the Game. Retrieved from https://www.newsweek.com

48 (2015, October 17). Newsweek Special Edition, Jordan: 30 Years Since MJ Changed the Game. Retrieved from https://www.newsweek.com

48-49 Dweck, Carol S. (2006), Ibid.

49 Roenigk, Alyssa via ESPN (2018, February 14), Ibid.

49 *"I wanted him to stop snowboarding."* Roenigk, Alyssa via ESPN (2018, February 14), Ibid.

50 *"We never doubted him we were just afraid."* Roenigk, Alyssa via ESPN (2018, February 14), Ibid.

54 Bandini, Paolo (2018, February 5) I Have Daily Struggles https://www.theguardian.com

54 Dweck, Carol S. (2006), Ibid.

55 Dweck, Carol S. (2006), Ibid.

56 Dweck, Carol S. (2006), Ibid.

56 Dweck, Carol S. (2006), Ibid.

Chapter 3:

63 *"I did horrible,"* he recalled. *"I crashed in the first half hour of practice and was out the whole contest. That was a huge eye-opener for me and I realized how tall of a ladder I had to climb."* McNair Brian (2015, August 5). Mount Alberts Brett Rheeder Looking for the Triple Crown. Retrieved from https://www.YorkRegion.com

63 McNair, Brian (2015, August 5). Mount Alberts Brett Rheeder Looking for the Triple Crown. Retrieved from https://www.YorkRegion.com

63 Rheeder, Brett. Retrieved from https://www.crankworx.com

63 *"It was my second time back in Les Deux Alps, since my back injury there in*

2013, and also the first Crankworx I won where none of my competitors messed up or crashed. It was a straight-up win." Brett Rheeder. Retrieved from https://www.crankworx.com

64 Redmond, Derek (2012, July 27). Derek Redmond: The Day That Changed my Life. Retrieved from https://www.DailyMail.com

64 *"You're a champion, you've got nothing to prove."* Redmond, Derek (2012, July 27). Derek Redmond: The Day That Changed my Life. Retrieved from https://www.DailyMail.com

65-66 Duckworth, Angela (2016). Grit: The Power of Passion and Perseverance, 1st ed., New York, NY. :Scribner (An imprint of Simon and Schuster)

66 Duckworth, Angela (2016), Ibid.

66 *"grit is mutable"* Duckworth, Angela (2016), Ibid.

66 McNair, Brian (2015, August 5). Mount Alberts Brett Rheeder Looking for the Triple Crown. Retrieved from https://www.YorkRegion.com

67 *"continued effort to do or achieve something despite difficulties, failure or opposition."* Retrieved from https://www.merriam-webster.com

67 Dweck, Carol S. (2006), Ibid.

69 Redmond, Derek (2012, July 27). Derek Redmond: The Day That Changed my Life. Retrieved from https://www.DailyMail.com

70 Barker, Eric (2015, January 31). A Navy Seal Explains 8 Secrets to Grit and Resilience – Barking Up the Wrong Tree. Retrieved from https://theweek.com

73 Dweck, Carol S. (2006), Ibid.

74 Brodesser-Akner, Taffy (2018). Tonya Harding Would Like Her Apology Now. Retrieved from https://www.nytimes.com

74 Brodesser-Akner, Taffy (2018). Tonya Harding Would Like Her Apology

Now. Retrieved from https://www.nytimes.com

74 1994 Winter Olympics: Tonya Harding Finishes 8th in Women's Figure Skating. (1994, February 25). Retrieved from https://www.oregonlive.com

77 Barker, Eric (2015, January 31). A Navy Seal Explains 8 Secrets to Grit and Resilience – Barking Up the Wrong Tree. Retrieved from https://theweek.com

Chapter 4:

80 Barker, Eric (2015, January 31). A Navy Seal Explains 8 Secrets to Grit and Resilience – Barking Up the Wrong Tree. Retrieved from https://theweek.com

82 Fields, Bill (2006, May 12). The Genius of Earl Woods. Retrieved from https://www. Golf digest.com

Chapter 5:

100 *"It's not important where the puck is but where the puck is going-"* Kirby, Jason (2014, September 24). Why Businesspeople Won't Stop Using That Gretzky Quote. Retrieved from https://www.macleans.ca/economy/

102 Feigley, D.A. (2006). Overcoming Psychological Blocking in Gymnastics. Technique, 38(8), 12-16. Retrieved from http://www.usagymlegacy.org

104 *"different psychological responses are incompatible with each other."* Wolpe, James (1968, October). Psychotherapy by Reciprocal Inhibition. Retrieved from https://www.springer.com

106 MacKenzie, David (2009, August 7). Phil Mickelson Mental Game: Why Mental Game Rehearsal is Important. Retrieved from http://my.golfstateof-mind.com

106 Fogg, Andrew. (2009). The Secrets of Hypnotic Golf. Lulu.com

106 Lazarus, Clifford N. (2013, January 29). The Truth About Hypnosis. Retrieved from https://www.psychologytoday.com

106 Bell, Vaughn (2016, April 20). The Trippy State Between Wakefulness and Sleep. Retrieved from https://www.theatlantic.com

Chapter 6:

112-113 Mitrosilis, Teddy (2015, April 9). Nine Shots that Remind Us How Incredible Tiger Woods Can Be. Retrieved from https://www.foxsports.com

113 Shaffer, Jonas (2018, March 21). Michael Phelps Won the Most Olympic Medals Ever, But He wasn't Dominant Enough for ESPN. Retrieved from https://www.baltimoresun.com

113 *"I think that part is pretty easy - - it's hard work, dedication, not giving up"*, Scutti, Susan (2018, January 20). Michael Phelps: 'I am extremely thankful that I did not take my life'. Retrieved from https://www.cnn.com

114 Svrluga, Barry (2008, August 9). Phelp's Head Is Above Water. Retrieved from https://www.washingtonpost.com

114 Garavan, H (1998). Serial Attention within working memory. Memory and Cognition. 26:263-276; McElree, B. (1998). Attended and non-attended states in working memory: Accessing categorized structures. Journal of Memory and Language, 38, 225-252

114 Raghunathan, Raj Ph.D. (2013, October 10). How Negative is Your "Mental Chatter"?. Retrieved from https://www.psychologytoday.com

117-118 Buchanan, Justin (2016, July 28). Albert Bandura:Self Efficacy for Agentic Positive Psychology. Retrieved from https://positivepsychologyprogram.com

118 Merriam Webster Dictionary. Retrieved from https://www.merriam-webster.com

118 Merriam Webster Dictionary. Retrieved from https://www.merriam-webster.com

119 Buchanan, Justin (2016, July 28). Albert Bandura:Self Efficacy for Agentic Positive Psychology. Retrieved from https://positivepsychologyprogram.com

119 *"It is essential to have a mentor that is knowledgeable and practices what they preach."* Buchanan, Justin (2016, July 28). Albert Bandura:Self Efficacy for Agentic Positive Psychology. Retrieved from https://positivepsychologyprogram.com

120 Buchanan, Justin (2016, July 28). Albert Bandura:Self Efficacy for Agentic Positive Psychology. Retrieved from https://positivepsychologyprogram.com

121 Buchanan, Justin (2016, July 28). Albert Bandura:Self Efficacy for Agentic Positive Psychology. Retrieved from https://positivepsychologyprogram.com

Chapter 7:

124 Friedman, Hilary Levey (2013, September 20). When Did Competitive Sports Take Over American Childhood?. Retrieved from https://www.theatlantic.com

124 MacDonald, Mikka (2016, September 15). Being a College Athlete requires sacrifices. Safety and Equal Access Shouldn't be Among Them. Retrieved from https://www.aspeninstitute.org

125 *"[Student-athletes] are coming into college now with so much more experience than a typical high school kid would have, because they have been playing quarterback 12 months out the year, they have been going to summer camp, they've been going to an IMG academy [a preparatory boarding school and sports training institution]."* MacDonald, Mikka (2016, September 15). Being a College Athlete requires sacrifices. Safety and Equal Access Shouldn't be Among Them. Retrieved from https://www.aspeninstitute.org

125 MacDonald, Mikka (2016, September 15). Being a College Athlete requires sacrifices. Safety and Equal Access Shouldn't be Among Them. Retrieved from https://www.aspeninstitute.org

126 *"As more and more children specialize in a single sport at a younger age,*

research suggests that they face a higher risk of overuse injuries from training, as well as an increase in potential for stress and burnout, according to a clinical report from the American Academy of Pediatrics." (2016, August 29). AAP Clinical report: Young Children Risk Injury in Single-Sport Specialization. Retrieved from https://www.aap.org

126 (2016, August 29). AAP Clinical report: Young Children Risk Injury in Single-Sport Specialization. Retrieved from https://www.aap.org

126 Miner, Julianna W. (2016, June 1). Why 70 Percent of Kids Quit Sports by Age 13. Retrieved from: https://www.washingtonpost.com

127 "*The ultimate goal of sports is for kids to have fun and learn lifelong physical activity skills. We want kids to have more time for deliberate play, where they can just go out and play with their friends and have fun.*" Brenner, Joel S. (2016, September). Sport Specialization and Intensive Training in Young Athletes. Retrieved from https://www.pediatirics.aappublications.org

127 Brenner, Joel S. (2016, September). Sport Specialization and Intensive Training in Young Athletes. Retrieved from https://www.pediatirics.aappublications.org

127-128 "*the intentional and voluntary nature of informal sport games designed to maximize inherent enjoyment.*" Brenner, Joel S. (2016, September). Sport Specialization and Intensive Training in Young Athletes. Retrieved from https://www.pediatirics.aappublications.org

128 Brenner, Joel S. (2016, September). Sport Specialization and Intensive Training in Young Athletes. Retrieved from https://www.pediatirics.aappublications.org

129 "*What controls your decisions are the patterns and habits you create in your life.*" Dill, Katherine (2017, May 23). Tony Robbins: Only you can create the life you deserve–here's how. Retrieved from: https://www.cnbc.com

Chapter 8:

135 Sobel, Jason (2017, August 12). Jason Day Quadruple-Bogeys His Final Hole to Fall 7 Back. Retrieved from https://www.espn.com

135 "...*I'm like, 'My game is not where it should be. I'm not doing the right things on the course. I really haven't had the greatest year.' You're not panicking or anything. You're just wondering why. You're up at night thinking about, 'Ok what do I need to do to get back to winning form?' I think once I minimize the distractions in my life and can focus more on playing golf and focus, and single-focus on golf, then everything will take care of itself.*" Sobel, Jason (2017, August 12). Jason Day Quadruple-Bogeys His Final Hole to Fall 7 Back. Retrieved from https://www.espn.com

137 "...*you don't rise to the occasion, you sink to the level of your training...*" Schrage, Michael (2015, May 28). How the Navy SEALs Train for Leadership Excellence. Retrieved from: https://www.hbr.org

137 Barker, Eric (2015, January 31). A Navy Seal Explains 8 Secrets to Grit and Resilience – Barking Up the Wrong Tree. Retrieved from https://theweek.com

137 "*Repetition is the mother of skill.*" Robbins, Anthony (1991). Awaken the Giant Within, First Fireside Ed., New York, NY.: Simon and Shuster

Chapter 9:

146 "*gifted individuals are those who demonstrate outstanding levels of aptitude (defined as an exceptional ability to reason and learn) or competence (documented performance or achievement in top 10% or rarer) in one or more domains...*" National Association for Gifted Children (2010, March). Redefining Giftedness for a New Century. Retrieved from https://www.nagc.org

146 "*who demonstrate professional abilities before age 10*" Roos, David (2014, October). 10 Child Prodigies. Retrieved from https://www.science.howstuffworks

147 "...*in the fixed mindset, both positive and negative labels can mess with*

your mind. When you are given a positive label you're afraid of losing it, and when you're hit with a negative label, you're afraid of deserving it." Dweck, Carol (2006), Ibid.

147 *"When people are in a growth mindset, the stereotype doesn't disrupt their performance. The growth mindset disrupts the stereotype and makes people better able to fight back. They don't believe in permanent inferiority. And if they are behind – well, then they'll work harder and try to catch up."* Carol (2006), Ibid.

147 Quackenbush, Eric (2009, February 15). The Unembellished story of Vince Papale. Retrieved from https://www.bleacherreport.com

147 Moss, Richard (2018, October 10). What Happened to Jim Morris from "The Rookie". Retrieved from https://www.peupdateblog.com

150 Miner, Julianna (2016, June 1). Why 70 Percent of Kids Quit Sports by Age 13. Retrieved from: https://www.washingtonpost.com

151 Brenner, Joel S. (2016, September). Sport Specialization and Intensive Training in Young Athletes. Retrieved from https://www.pediatirics.aappublications.org

151 (2016, August 29). AAP Clinical report: Young Children Risk Injury in Single-Sport Specialization. Retrieved from https://www.aap.org

Chapter 10:

156 *"A person overly involved in their children's life"* Merriam Webster Dictionary. Retrieved from https://www.merriam-webster.com

158 Diaz, Jaime (2016, December 9). After Split with Lydia Ko, David Leadbetter Cautions Her About Meddlesome Parents. Retrieved from https:// www.golfdigest.com

159 (2017, July 25). Mass. HS Basketball Coach Returns After Resigning Over Parents. Retrieved from https://coachad.com

159 *"At the end of the day, the reason I am resigning is because of parents."* (2017, July 25). Mass. HS Basketball Coach Returns After Resigning Over Parents. Retrieved from https://coachad.com

159 *"Parents have taken the fun and enjoyment right out of it [coaching]."* (2017, July 25). Mass. HS Basketball Coach Returns After Resigning Over Parents. Retrieved from https://coachad.com

159 Dweck, Carol (2006), Ibid.

159-160 *"Not a recipe for success in business, where taking on challenges, showing persistence, and admitting and correcting mistakes are essential."*, Ibid.

164 *"1- Every human movement, thought, or feeling is a precisely timed electrical signal traveling through a chain of neurons – a circuit of nerve fibers. 2- Myelin is the insulation that wraps these nerve fibers and increases signal strength, speed and accuracy. 3 – The more we fire a particular circuit, the more Myelin optimizes that circuit and the stronger, faster and more fluent our movements and thoughts become."* Coyle, Daniel (2009). The Talent Code, 1st. Ed., New York, NY: Bantam Books, 32

164 *"Struggle is not optional – it's neurologically required: in order to get your skill circuit to fire optimally, you must by definition fire the circuit sub-optimally; you must make mistakes and pay attention to those mistakes; you must slowly teach your circuit. You must also keep firing your circuit – i.e. practicing – in order to keep Myelin functioning properly."* Coyle, Daniel (2009). The Talent Code, 1st. Ed., New York, NY: Bantam Books, 32

Chapter 11:

170 *"It's in our moments of decision that your destiny is shaped"*, Robbins, Anthony (1991). Awaken the Giant Within, First Fireside Ed., New York, NY.: Simon and Shuster

170 Robbins, Anthony (1991), Ibid.

171 Lecky, P. (1945). Self-Consistency: A theory of personality (J.F. Taylor, Ed.). Island Press.

172 "For every action, there is an equal and opposite reaction." Newton's Third Law. Retrieved from https//www.physicsclassroom.com

174 Taylor, J.B. (2006). My Stroke of Insight: A Brain Scientist's Personal Journey. Penguin Random House, LLC.

174 Garavan, H. (1998). Serial attention with working memory. Memory and Cognition. 26:263-276; McElree, B. (1998). Attended and non-attended states in working memory: Accessing categorized structures. Journal of Memory and Language, 38, 225-252

175 "You don't dance to get to the other side of the floor." Watts, Allen (n.d.). Retrieved from: https//www.books.google.com

Chapter 12:

185 Trinko, Katrina (2018, February 11). Listen to Nick Foles, Not Social Media. Failure Helps You Succeed. Retrieved from https://www.usatoday.com

185-186 Trinko, Katrina (2018, February 11). Listen to Nick Foles, Not Social Media. Failure Helps You Succeed. Retrieved from https://www.usatoday.com

Checklists:

201 Schneiderman, N., Ironson, G., & Siegel, S. D. (2005). Stress and health: psychological, behavioral, and biological determinants. Annual review of clinical psychology, 1, 607–628.doi:10.1146/annurev.clinpsy.1.102803.144141

203 Mindset Works, Inc. (2017). Growth Mindset Tools and Resources to Transform School Culture. Leader Kit, 137. Retrieved from

204 Dweck, Carol S. (2006) Mindset, 1st. ed., New York, NY.: Random House, Inc.

CHECKLISTS AND TABLES

Checklists of Critical Points

Chapter 1: Temperament. Understand your parenting style and child's temperament to foster the most nurturing environment.

1. Understand your parenting style: authoritative, authoritarian, permissive, or neglectful.

2. Understand your child's temperament. Are they "slow-to-warm," "easy," or "difficult?" Know that there are no bad temperaments. Learning what temperament your child tends toward will help you establish the most nurturing environment for them.

3. Understanding "goodness of fit". How your child's temperament matches or mismatches with their environment will impact the productivity of their growth. Below is a table of signs and symptoms that the child's temperament is not fitting well with their current environment.

Table 3.1. Selected Signs and Symptoms of Stress

Selected Signs and Symptoms of Stress		
Behavioral	**Physiological**	**Psychological**
• Difficulty sleeping or Sleeping too much • Angry Outbursts • Consistently performs better in practice/training than in competition • Social Withdrawal • Poor Decision Making • Substance abuse	• Feeling ill, Upset stomach • Cold, clammy hands • Profuse sweating • Headaches • Increased muscle tension or pain • Chest pain • Altered appetite • Fatigue	• Lack of motivation • Restlessness • Lack of motivation or focus • Feeling Overwhelmed • Irritability or anger • Negative self-talk • Uncontrollable intrusive and negative thoughts or images • Self doubt

Source: Schneiderman, N., Ironson, G., & Siegel, S. D. (2005)

Chapter 2: Mindset. Develop a growth mindset with a focus on the journey, not the results. Help your athlete see failure as an opportunity to grow and learn, not a place of shame and disappointment.

1. Know your mindset. Know your child's mindset. See the chart "Growth vs. Fixed Mindset" below.

2. Learn how to become growth minded. See chart "Four Steps Toward a Growth Mindset" below.

3. If your child has a fixed mindset, turn that around to a growth mindset. This will help them to learn and grow, but it is also critical to developing grit and self-efficacy.

4. Remember, to develop a growth mindset you need time, repetition, patience, and an overall change to how *you* address failure.

5. What is your vocabulary? Your athlete's? Use growth-minded words.

6. Praise effort not accomplishment. Recognize effort, not results.

7. Praise must be kept specific, not expressed in generalities. Say: I like the way you _____.

8. Encourage your athlete to take appropriate challenges.

Growth Mindset vs. Fixed Mindset

Growth Mindset	Fixed Mindset
___ Other people's success is inspiring.	___ Other people's success is threatening.
___ Everyone can succeed.	___ I wasn't born to succeed.
___ Failure makes me grow.	___ Failure highlights my limits and tells me that I am no good.
___ Feedback is constructive.	
___ I like to try new things.	___ Feedback is personal.
___ If others can do it, I can!	___ I do not like to try new things.
___ Takes responsibility for failure.	___ It's everyone else's fault.
___ I can learn anything I want to.	___ Knowledge is limited.
___ When I'm frustrated, I persevere.	___ I'm either good at it, or I'm not.
___ My efforts and attitude determine everything.	___ When I'm frustrated, I give up.
	___ My abilities determine everything.
___ Tell me I try hard.	___ Tell me I'm smart.
___ I want to challenge myself.	___ I don't like to be challenged.

Source: Mindset Works, Inc. (2017).

Four Steps Towards a Growth Mindset

Follow these simple steps to help shift from a fixed to a growth mindset.

Step 1. Identify your fixed mindset voice.

Listen to the little voice in your brain which is telling you how you fell and what you think about a certain situation.

This voice would say things like:
- I will never be able to do this.
- I have never done it, so won't know what to do next.
- Last time, trying something new ended up in a disaster.
- Others have much more experience which I don't have.

Step 2. Realize that you have a choice.

Expand your mind and offer yourself the contrary of what your mind is thinking at a certain point in time

Example phrases that you can apply to re-frame your mind.

- I'm not born to be successful → I can work hard on improving my skills even if I am not good enough yet.
- Last time I failed at this. → I failed at this before, but I learned from it and that should allow me to be better this time.
- I hate being criticized. → Criticism can help me see the situation differently and might help me change my perspective.
- I can't speak Chinese. → I can't speak Chinese, yet.

Step 3. Make the Decision.

- Encourage yourself to use growth mindset thoughts and voice.

Step 4. Take Consistent action.

- Commit to the challenge wholeheartedly, learn from setbacks and try again

Source: Dweck, Carol S. (2006)

Chapter 3: Grit. We define grit in the book as passion, perseverance, and low need for positive reinforcement. If you work on these attributes that make up grit throughout your child's life but especially in sports, they will develop grit.

1. Encourage development of passion. You can't give passion, but you can foster it by demonstrating it in your life and by giving encouragement.

2. Establish a growth-minded environment to promote perseverance. Let your child see failure as a growth opportunity and to not fear but embrace challenges.

3. Model grit in how you approach failures. The way you handle adversity within your own life should demonstrate grit.

4. Use specific feedback focused on constructive reinforcement. Do not compliment or ridicule with overly positive or overly negative comments. Don't speak in generalities. Give specific feedback that is constructive and encouraging.

Chapter 4: Goal Setting involves three levels: outcome, performance, and process. Instill goal setting by using all three levels to increase performance. Make goal setting a process your child uses in all areas of their life.

1. Talk to your athlete about their goals.

2. Encourage the athlete to set goals using the three levels: outcome, performance, and process. Outcome is the overall goal. Performance is how the athlete will measure if the goal is achieved. Process is the specific training for the athlete to achieve that goal.

3. Guide your athlete through the goal setting process to be sure goals are both attainable and measurable.

4. Set specific timelines for goal achievement and reviews. Once one goal is met, restart the process to address a new goal. If the goal is not met, discuss why and then revisit the goal and adjust as necessary.

Chapter 5: Practice –All practices should start with a goal. "Time is important, focus is more important, and goals are most important." Practicing with a goal will allow for a more productive practice.

2. Follow deep dedicated practice to embed skills: drill down to the most basic skill to focus on and build from there. Revisit our discussion on block training.

2. Increase focus through awareness training techniques described in detail in the chapter.

3. Practice mental game techniques to improve performance: attentional shifting, imagery, mental prompts, and hypnosis.

Chapter 6: Self-Efficacy starts with the integration of trust and faith in one's skills. Trust is based on proof and proof is derived through practice and play. The athlete should always assess their abilities focused on their execution, never on winning.

1. Continue to develop growth mindedness and grit.

2. Stop focusing on feelings and telling your kids to be confident. Keep the critiques specific while encouraging them to grow and learn.

3. Practice is critical to build trust and faith in their abilities.

4. Provide an environment that demonstrates passion and perseverance.

5. Keep feedback specific and growth minded.

Chapter 7: Assessing Readiness. Knowing when your child is ready for more elite teams or specialization.

1. Know your child.

2. Listen to your child.

3. Know the risks of specialization too early as detailed in the chapter.

4. Delay specialization until appropriate for your athlete.

5. Encourage kids to play multiple sports.

6. Monitor, without hovering, over all training and coaching to be sure it's age and skill appropriate.

7. Rest is important. One or two days a week should be sport-free, and kids should take about 3 months away from each sport.

8. Make time for deliberate play.

9. Keep the fun in sports.

Chapter 8: Pressure

1. Stay growth minded in your words and actions.

2. Keep improving the athlete's grit through growth-minded words and specific feedback.

3. Keep improving the athlete's self-efficacy by encouraging the athlete to practice and establish proof in their abilities.

4. Proper training reduces pressure.

5. Use imagery techniques detailed in the chapter to help the athlete perform well under pressure.

Chapter 9: Hidden Dangers

1. Stop labeling.

2. Do not follow the pack.

3. Identify burnout.

4. Quitting isn't failure. It's just a change.

Chapter 10: Extreme Parenting

1. Identify the degree to which you control your child's life.

2. Allow for age-appropriate independence.

3. Use growth-minded language.

4. Have more conversations, and five fewer lectures.

Chapter 11: Support from the Sidelines

1. Determine your master motive.

2. Talk with the athlete to see what they need from you.

3. Set goals for yourself as a supporter from the sidelines.

4. Be an active listener and hear what your athlete is telling you.

5. Look for non-verbal cues to understand your athlete.

6. Use imagery to help you set goals.

7. Use reciprocal imagery to stop your anger within the 90 seconds.

8. Practice mindfulness. Be present.

9. Avoid confrontations with coaches and other parents at games or practice. Keep conversations calm and private.

ABOUT THE AUTHORS

Dr. Nick Molinaro has worked in the arena of performance psychology for over 30 years with middle-school aged children through professional and Olympic athletes in all sports. His client list includes athletes/players from NASCAR, NBA, NFL, AFL, CFL, Olympic Gold and Silver Medalists, members of US Ski and Gymnastic Teams, 2016 Ice Skating and X-Games. However, Dr. Nick is mostly known for his work with professional and amateur golfers. He's worked with players on PGA, LPGA, Web.com, Champions, Symetra, Mackenzie, PGA Asian, PGA Germany, PGA South American, LET, Mini, and Minor tours. As well As The Golf Channels's Big Break Contestants.

Dr. Nick has also made guest appearances of both television and radio for such shows as Fox5 News, Fox5 Sports, The Golf Channel, SiriusXM PGA Tour Radio, SiriusXM NBA Radio, ESPN Sports Radio,CBS Sports Radio. He is also a contributing writer for Michael Breed Golf Academy News Letter and Womensgolf.com.

In addition, Dr. Nick works with individuals, teams, and/or coaching staffs of 31 college conferences across Divisions I,II, and III. For a complete list of the conferences Dr. Nick is affiliated with, please see below. He also serves on the advisory board of the North Jersey Fellowship of Christian Athletes.

Co-author, Celeste Romano, is the founder and head of Creative Licensing Publishing, LLC., a writing consulting firm and a hybrid-publisher for the Indie author. She has done freelance writing for online magazines about raising her two sons, Alex and Zach. She has also written a novel for middle-school aged children.

List of College Conferences

Divison I
Big 12 Conference
Patriot League
Pac-12 Conference
Big 10
SCC
ACC
SEC East Division
SEC West Division
Atlantic 10
American Athletic Conference (AAC)
Metro Atlantic Athletic Conference (MAAC)
Big East Conference
America East Conference
Atlantic Sun Conference
Sun Belt Conference Football
Northeast Conference
Southern Conference (SoCon)

Division II
Northeast 10 Conference
Sunshine State Conference

Division III
Middle Atlantic Conferences (MAC)
MAC Commonwealth
MAC Freedom
Centenial Conference
New England Small College Athletic Conference (NESCAC)
New England Women's and Men's Athletic Conference (NEWMAC)
New Jersey Athletic Conference (NJAC)
Liberty League
Old Dominion Athletic Conference
Commonwealth Coast Conference
USA South Athletic Conference

Made in the
USA
Middletown, DE